D0847861

the friendship book

WENDY L. MOSS, PHD

Magination Press • Washington, DC
American Psychological Association

This book is dedicated to my special friends—Cindy, Donald, Marilyn, Penny, and Vicky. I have loved going through the journey of the decades alongside each of you!—WLM

Books for Kids From the
American Psychological Association

Copyright © 2021 Wendy L. Moss. Published in 2021 by Magination Press, an imprint of the American Psychological Association. All rights reserved. Except as permitted under the United States Copyright Act of 1976, no part of this publication may be reproduced or distributed in any form or by any means, or stored in a database or retrieval system, without the prior written permission of the publisher.

Magination Press is a registered trademark of the American Psychological Association. Order books at maginationpress.org, or call 1-800-374-2721.

Book design by Rachel Ross
Printed by Phoenix Color, Hagerstown, MD

Library of Congress Cataloging-in-Publication Data
Names: Moss, Wendy (Wendy L.), author.
Title: The friendship book / Wendy L. Moss, PhD.
Description: Washington, DC : Magination Press, [2021] | Summary: "Figure out what you want out of your friendships, how to be a good friend, how to resolve conflicts, and much more"—Provided by publisher.
Identifiers: LCCN 2020025378 (print) | LCCN 2020025379 (ebook) | ISBN 9781433832291 (hardcover) | ISBN 9781433834677 (ebook)
Subjects: LCSH: Friendship in children—Juvenile literature. | Friendship—Juvenile literature.
Classification: LCC BF723.F68 M67 2021 (print) | LCC BF723.F68 (ebook) | DDC 177/.62—dc23
LC record available at https://lccn.loc.gov/2020025378
LC ebook record available at https://lccn.loc.gov/2020025379
Manufactured in the United States of America
10 9 8 7 6 5 4 3 2 1

Table of Contents

Introduction

Many different factors contribute to having close friendships, and there are many different things you can do to maintain them. That's what this book is all about: making friends, keeping friends, and being a good friend to others.

Friendships can help you to feel accepted, allow you to share experiences, give you reasons to laugh and smile, and help you to feel connected. Friends can also be an important support system when you need to rely on people you can trust. Some people make friends easily, while others sometimes struggle. Even if you are an interesting, kind, friendly person, you may still find that you want more friends than you currently have.

In this book, you will read about the definition of a friend, how you can make sure that you are ready to be a good friend, and the potential joys and complications of having a best friend. In addition, you will have an opportunity to think about times when you may want to be alone; ways to compromise, survive disagreements, and navigate the challenges of friendships; and the pros and cons of socializing over social media.

Throughout this book, you will get the chance to read about how other kids have made and kept friends. However, in order to protect the privacy of specific children, these examples are summaries of many different children's stories. They are not meant to describe situations faced by one specific person.

On your journey toward knowing how to make and keep friends, take time to think about what makes you special and what you like about yourself. If you take pride in how you act, the things you do, or the talents you have, compliment yourself! As you start making new friends, consider what you want your friends to appreciate in you. Then think about what you value in a friendship and how you can be a good friend to someone else.

Best of luck in finding, keeping, and enjoying your friendships!

1

SEEKING FRIENDS

HAVE YOU EVER THOUGHT ABOUT WHY YOU WANT to have friends? Do you know what you want out of a friendship? Lots of kids may imagine that a good friend will have the same interests as them or think just like them. They may want friends who have a similar sense of humor and will want to spend a lot of time with them. Other kids might find that it's fun to have friends who are different from themselves. They may want to seek out new and exciting experiences with friends who are more adventurous, more popular, or more knowledgeable about certain topics. Many kids seek friends who can be trusted, who they can confide in, and with whom they can share private thoughts.

Spending time with good friends can be a wonderful experience, but there might be times when you prefer to be alone, or even times in your life when you're not that interested in making friends. You may (or may not) be surprised to learn that it's normal to prefer being by yourself sometimes. When you're alone, you can sing, dance, read your favorite books, or do other activities just because you feel like it. You don't have to worry about what another person wants to do. When you're ready to be social again, you can reach out to your friends. It's important to nurture your friendships and find a comfortable balance between alone time and friend time.

In this chapter, you will get the chance to think about what you may want from a friendship, how much of your free time you would like to spend with friends, and what kinds of things you might enjoy doing with others. You will also learn about the circles of people in your life. Before reading further, though, try taking the quiz on the next page. You can't fail it! It's just an opportunity to think about what you want in a friendship and how you react to other people.

Quiz

1. **You don't have much in common with the popular kids in your grade, but you want to be popular, too. So you:**

   a. pretend to be just like them to fit in and make more friends.

   b. try to find one thing that you and one of these kids both enjoy and begin to hang out together doing this one activity.

   c. decide that you should try to make friends with kids who you are more comfortable with, and with whom you share the same interests, whether they are popular or not.

2. **You want to spend lots of time with friends. You think that it might be fun to be close friends with a certain kid in your grade, but you know that the person is very busy. Do you:**

   a. give up on that potential friendship because you only want a friend who can spend lots of time with you?

   b. try to get together sometimes with this person, but don't think a close friendship is likely because you aren't spending time together or connecting on social media every day?

   c. decide that you want to become friends, even if you can't spend lots of time together, and you look for other friends to fill the rest of your free time?

3. **How ready are you to be friends with others who want to spend time doing things that you you don't think you will enjoy?**

   a. I'm looking for a friend who only likes to do things that I like to do.

   b. I know that I need to do some things that my friends want to do, even if I'm not interested. I'll do whatever my friends ask in order to be accepted.

   c. I know that I need to compromise sometimes and support my friends. But I also know that I don't want to be friends with anyone who won't accept me unless I do dangerous things or things that make me very uncomfortable.

4. **Laura wants all of her friends to be trustworthy so that she can share her personal thoughts and feelings with them. One day, Laura told a friend that she was going to try smoking. This friend told her own mother, who called Laura's mother. Laura felt betrayed and ended the friendship. What would you have done?**

   a. Definitely end the friendship! You won't ever be able to trust your friend again since she shared your secret.

   b. Talk with your friend and ask that she keep all your secrets.

   c. Calmly ask your friend why she shared your plan with her mother. You consider that she may actually be a good friend because she was worried about you.

5. Can you have different kinds of friends—some to share hobbies, some to study with, some to laugh with, and some to share secrets with?

a. You feel that a true friend is someone who you can share hobbies with, study with, laugh with, and confide in. If others don't fit that whole description, you don't want them as friends.

b. You are okay hanging out with friends who you don't share a lot in common with, but you want a best friend who is almost just like you.

c. You don't need your friends to be just like you. You think it's great to have friends who can share different interests with you. It's a great way to discover and do new things.

Quiz Results

If you answered mostly 'a,' then making friends might have created some stress for you in the past, as you tried to figure out how to be friends with kids who are somewhat different from yourself.

If you answered mostly 'b,' then you understand that even very good friends may not always share your same interests. It could be helpful for you to learn ways of handling situations when you and your friend want to do different activities or don't see things the same way.

If you answered mostly 'c,' then you probably already have a good idea about how to make and keep friends. But keep reading—you may still pick up some important tips!

Jeremy

Jeremy, age 10, had lots of hobbies and he liked sports. He felt lucky that he had friends who he could share these different activities with at different times. He told his mom, "I don't expect one kid to be just like me and enjoy everything that I like. It's great if they enjoy one thing, or a few things, and it's definitely important that they are nice and stand up for other kids instead of being mean and insulting to people."

Jeremy played hockey with Ramon, baseball with Stephen, and basketball with Stephen and Zev. He liked to joke around with Maggie and write rap songs and act out plays with Rebecca, Pauline, and Mateo. Sometimes, Jeremy did things with his friends that weren't his favorite, but he still had fun participating and making his friends happy. He was proud that he chose friends who shared his values of kindness and respect. His friends didn't pressure him to do things that made him uncomfortable and they all treated each other well. He had fun with his friends and felt supported and accepted!

- ° If you were Jeremy, would you be friends with someone who shared similar interests, but disrespected you?
- ° What would you do if your friend asked you to join an activity that's not one of your favorites?

Friendship Checklist

Once you know what you are looking for in a friend, it can be easier to find friends who want the same things you do. Luckily, you can have many different kinds of friends! Below, you will find lists of things you might look for in a friend. The first list gives you examples of activities that you may want to share with friends. The second list gives you examples of the kinds of personality traits you may seek in your friends. As you read through both lists, write down the characteristics that are important to you on a separate piece of paper. By the end of this activity, you'll hopefully have a list of qualities to look for when making friends.

Activities That You Want Your Friend to Enjoy:

Some of my favorite sports

Doing art projects

Doing well in school

Reading and talking about books

Going to the movies

Theatre, singing, or dancing

Playing board games

Baking or cooking

Crafting like sewing or knitting

Being in clubs at school

Relaxing and talking about many things

Playing video games

Working to make the world a more positive place

Using social media

Talking about feelings

Music

Being imaginative

Spending time outdoors

Qualities That You Seek in a Friend:

Outgoing

Shy or quiet

Usually seems relaxed and calm

Usually has high energy

Good sense of humor

Likes spreading kindness

Respectful to others

Confident

Your parent would like this person

Cares about what others think and feel

Likes being part of a group

Likes hanging out one-on-one

Accepting of your opinions

Knows how to compromise

Trustworthy

Avoids spreading rumors

Did you create your own list? Maybe you enjoy some activities or appreciate some qualities that aren't on this list. Feel free to add them! After all, it's your list. You may find one person who fits everything on your list. However, like Jeremy, you may want to connect with a bunch of different kids who share just some of the interests and personality traits that are important to you.

No matter what interests or qualities you seek in a friend, there are a few key things everyone should keep in mind when making new friends.

- Always make sure that they have the same major values as you, such as how they treat others and how they treat you.

- Spend some time thinking about whether they would make you comfortable or uncomfortable.

- The friends you choose should respect you. Make sure that you feel good about yourself when you're with your friends and that your friends help you to feel more confident in yourself as they remind you of your talents, abilities, or accomplishments.

- Think about whether you can respect that other person. Does this person care about others? Do you feel good about being associated with this potential friend?

- Another person's personality can actually be more important than the person's areas of interest when you pick someone to get to know better. Why? A kind and respectful friend is easier to trust!

Now you know more about the kind of friend you're seeking! Next, how do you figure out if someone has the interests or traits on your list if you don't know each other well? Watch, listen, and learn. Pay attention to how kids act when they are joking around. Are they making fun of others or just having fun and laughing? You can learn a lot about others by what they say to other kids or to their teacher. Are they polite in the way they speak? Or are they rude or self-absorbed?

Be a detective. Every day, kids show who they are by how they act and how they treat friends as well as those who aren't friends.

Now it's time to figure out how you like to socialize (spend time with friends). Thinking about this may help you to find friends who you're likely to be comfortable around.

How You Socialize

When you want to find friends, think about how you like to socialize. This can help you to find other kids who want to connect with you in the same way that you want to connect with them. Being comfortable the first few times you talk with someone can be a great way to start the journey toward becoming friends. Of course, sometimes it does take more time to get used to and get to know others.

To figure out how you like to socialize, try asking yourself the following questions:

- Are you looking for a friend to hang out with every day, or just once in a while?
- Are you okay hanging out with friends in a group, or are you looking for one-on-one friendships?
- Do you have time for a friend? If you are really busy with sports, clubs, family activities, and so on, maybe look for friends who go to the same activities.
- How important is it for you to connect with others over social media versus doing other activities together?
- Are you okay spending time with others who don't always feel or think the same way you do?

Having a lot in common is one good way to build a friendship. But it's also okay if you make friends with someone who is different.

The questions you just read are a guide to help you to figure out how you like to socialize, which can be helpful as you look for new friends. It's great if you end up making friends with someone who is very similar to you. Having a lot in common is a one good way to build a friendship. But it's also okay if you make friends with someone who is different. What might happen if you try to build a friendship with someone who, unlike you, prefers to hang out in groups instead of spending most of the time on social media or one-on-one? The friendship could work if you are both willing to compromise! Hopefully, you can both be flexible and sometimes socialize the way the other person is most comfortable. This kind of compromise and mutual respect can be a big help when starting friendships with those who are different from you. You might be surprised to find that socializing in a new way may be okay and even comfortable once you get used to it.

Circles of People in Your Life

There are circles of people in each of our lives who we are closer to than others. Imagine yourself with a bunch of circles around you. The center circle contains only you, since you probably trust and understand yourself most. The people closest to you are in your inner circle, or the circle just outside of your own. These are the people you're most comfortable with and trust a lot. As you go farther beyond those central circles, you're more likely to find people who might just be acquaintances, who you don't trust as much. The circle that someone is in isn't necessarily about who is nice and who isn't. It's more about who you feel most comfortable being with and who you trust most.

To better understand the circles of people in your life, try making a diagram of your own circles. Draw a very small circle in the middle

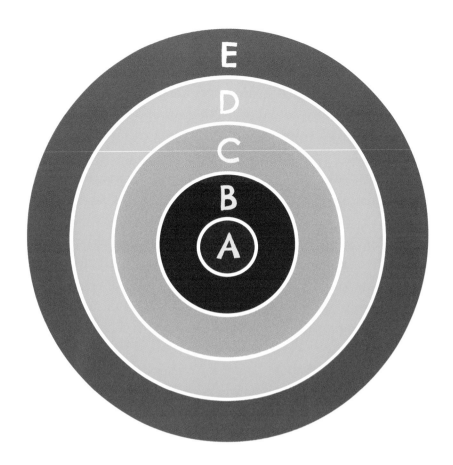

of a piece of paper and put the word 'ME' in the middle of it. You're with yourself all the time. You really understand how you feel and how you think. Hopefully, you also trust your judgment and feel confident in yourself. Let's call this circle "A."

Next, draw a slightly larger circle around the first one and call it "B." In this circle are the people (and even pets!) who you trust most in your life. If you feel sad or embarrassed, these are the people and pets who you generally turn to for support. You may put certain family members or best friends in this circle. You may also put your doctor or teacher in circle B, if these are people who you truly trust.

Now, draw a larger circle around circle B. This is circle C. In this circle, add people you like and trust, but not as much as you trust those in circle B. Perhaps you would put friends who you hang out with but who you don't really know well enough to fully trust.

There are two more circles in this example (but you can draw your own diagram with as many circles as you want). In circle D are your acquaintances. Acquaintances are people who you see but don't really know very well. Why list them, then? These are kids who you might like to get to know better and maybe try to become friends with over time.

The last circle is E. In this circle are kids who you want to keep your distance from right now. Perhaps some of these kids have picked on you or you saw these kids being unaccepting or even hurtful to others. Don't actually write down names in this circle. Names on paper could accidentally be seen by others and feelings could be hurt. Just remember who these kids are. Also, keep an open mind about moving kids from this group into circle D if you notice that you misjudged them or they're changing, and you want to give them a chance to become your friend.

Got it? Now think about how these circles can help you. Look at each circle and think about who you know and trust. Reviewing your chart might help you see who you already are friends with and who you might want to become closer to soon. Are there some kids in circles C and D, for instance, who you think might end up being good friends if you put in more effort to socialize with them? This is one way to use the information from these circles.

Over time, people may move in and out of some circles. For instance, imagine being friends with someone since kindergarten. You were best friends when you were five, but because of the ways you've both changed, you still like each other but aren't best friends anymore. It happens. As you update your chart, be careful not to knock a person down from circle B to circle E, for instance, just because of a disagreement. Instead, take the time to work on resolving your differences. Maybe that person will end up staying in circle B once you work it out. (In Chapter 4, you will learn how to work through conflicts without losing a friendship.)

As you look at these circles, feel free to discuss them with adults who you trust. It will let them get to know how you feel about

Emily

Emily, age 11, knew that she was often shy and quiet. She had one good friend, who she had known since nursery school. As they grew older, they attended different schools, but they still hung out when their families got together. Emily liked playing board games with this friend and liked connecting a few times a week through texting, e-mail, and social media.

Emily wanted to also become friends with some kids at school, but she thought it might be hard for her to hang out in large groups. So, she began thinking about which kids she could connect with on social media. Emily joined a group project for social studies. When the teacher asked students to form groups of three to work together online, Emily quietly asked Sarah if she could join her group. She knew Sarah a little because they were in the same art class. Sarah said that Emily could join her and Abby. Emily was nervous but also happy to be part of this group! They set up a group chat and Emily liked the fact that Sarah and Abby joked online. Emily got to know them and began to joke back. At school, Sarah and Abby began to say 'Hi' to her! Being in the same group was a great way for Emily to start friendships with Sarah and Abby. Emily began to work on getting to know them better in person!

- Do you have a way that you are most comfortable socializing?
- Can knowing how you are comfortable socializing help you to find a way to get to know other kids better?

people in your life. It's probably best not to share this information with other kids, though. If someone is in circle C, that kid may feel rejected because he's not your closest friend. If a person is in circle B, you might think it's okay to share the information. However, you would be asking a friend to keep a secret about who you like most and least. That's a big burden! Sometimes people prefer to just think about who would be in each circle instead of writing down names. This way no one's feelings are accidentally hurt if someone stumbles across the diagram.

Step-by-Step

Making and keeping friends who are right for you involves some thought and action. It's helpful to think about characteristics that you want in a friend. Try to be flexible so you don't overlook a potential friend who is different from you but would add to your life in a positive way. It's also important to take steps to make friends and think about how you can be a good friend to others; we'll cover both of these topics in the chapters ahead!

Call to Action

Take some time to think about who you trust and enjoy spending time with (perhaps look at the names of people who you listed in circles B and C). Why do you enjoy being around each of these people? Think about why you like them, in general. Once you know what characteristics they have that you like, you can begin to look for new friends who might have similar personalities or interests. While doing this, also try thinking about getting to know kids who are different from you or your current friends, who might provide you with new experiences or new ways to socialize. Just make sure anyone you hang out with is kind and supportive of you and you treat them the same way!

2

MAKING FRIENDS

SOME PEOPLE MAKE FRIENDS EASILY, BUT FOR OTHERS
it can be challenging. Some kids are comfortable hanging out and being themselves in a group, while others are shy or quiet and may prefer to watch rather than join in. Think about the friends you've made: how did you first get to know them? Did you become friends quickly, or did it take some time? Whatever your personality or social style, in this chapter, you will have an opportunity to think about how you've made friends in the past and how you can connect with others to begin building new friendships. Before you get started, try taking the quiz on the next page. It can help you to think about your approach to starting friendships.

Quiz

1. It's much harder to make friends if you spend most of your time at home and by yourself, without even connecting through social media. Right now:

    a. you are very comfortable being alone. Reaching out to others to make friends feels very stressful.

    b. you want to connect with other kids but aren't sure how to get started.

    c. you are motivated to make more friends and have already been thinking about what kind of friend you would like.

2. Have you observed how other kids are behaving and what they're doing around you? Some of them could be your future friends!

    a. No. I don't want to look like I'm nosy.

    b. I sometimes observe those around me, but I'm more focused on what I'm doing.

    c. Yes. It's helped me to figure out which kids I might like to get to know better.

3. Dimitri took a deep breath to relax, then asked Harold if he wanted to go to the fair on the weekend with Dimitri and his grandfather. Harold said, "I can't. I'm busy. Sorry!" If you were Dimitri would you:

    a. feel that Harold was clearly telling you that he didn't ever want to hang out, so you decide to never try to get together again?

b. believe that Harold is too busy to get together right now, but may still be a future friend?

c. feel that Harold may have either been busy that weekend or dislike going to fairs? You might decide to ask him what he's interested in, then see if he would like to do that activity together sometime soon.

4. **Think about the kind of person you want to be your friend. Are you looking for:**

a. a friend who is exactly like you so it's easy to spend time together?

b. a friendship where you get together only if your friend agrees to do what you like because you are uncomfortable trying new things?

c. a friend who shares some of the same interests, but also teaches you about new activities, treats you with respect, and helps you to feel good about yourself?

5. **When thinking about getting to know other kids, and other kids getting to know you, you:**

a. don't know what to do, or you would have done it already!

b. know that you should approach other kids but aren't sure how to start a conversation with them.

c. know there are things you can say and do (e.g., say "Hi" or compliment someone, or even casually ask what they like to do on weekends) that will help you get to know the kids who might be your future friends!

Quiz Results

If you answered mostly 'a,' then figuring out how to make new friends might create some anxiety or difficulty for you.

If you answered mostly 'b,' then you have some basic ideas of what you can do to start to get to know the kids you like.

If you answered mostly 'c,' then you may already have a very good idea about how to make friends, but you can still pick up some important tips as you keep reading!

Getting Ready

As you start on your journey to make new friends, it helps if you feel confident that you are a person worth knowing and having as a friend. When others notice your confidence, they may be curious about you and want to get to know you. (Being confident doesn't mean being arrogant. Be confident, but also be kind!)

If you feel good about yourself and believe you have good qualities that others would like, then you're already on your way to making friends. If you lack confidence, take some time to recognize all you have to offer as a friend. Try making a list of your abilities and special qualities. Everyone has special qualities! If this still doesn't boost your confidence, you may want to speak to a trusted adult (perhaps an adult that you listed in Chapter 1, in circle B) and ask for help. As you go through the process of building your confidence, remember your wonderful qualities so you can later share them with friends.

After you work on building your confidence, think about the kids you run into on a regular basis. You may want to look over names that you put into circle C. Would you like to try to be friends with any of these kids now? If so, you've already accomplished two important steps! You feel more confident, and you've identified who you want to get to know better.

Look Around

In this step, take some time to make a list of the activities or clubs you participate in. Then ask yourself if there are kids in these groups who you can add to your list of potential friends. Once you have your list, try to approach the kids you would like to get to know. Maybe you just end up sitting at the same table as those kids. Maybe you offer to share materials, or you work together on a project. There are many creative ways to start a conversation. If there are no kids in your activities who you want to approach, it's okay. Look back at the list you made in Chapter 1 of kids in circle C, or make a new list of kids from school or around your community who you might want to know better.

If you aren't involved in any clubs or activities, you may want to consider joining some. Think about what might overlap with your interests—sports, art, music? This may not be easy, especially if you are shy or more comfortable being alone, but you can try out a club or activity without making a long-term commitment. You can even speak with the adult in charge to find out more about it first. If it sounds like fun, try doing some positive self-talk to convince yourself to test it out. Positive self-talk is like giving yourself a pep talk; for example, saying, "I think I can!" or "Maybe I'll have a great time and something good will happen if I go!"

Clubs and activities are not the only places you can approach kids to make friends. You can speak with other kids on the school bus, in the lunchroom, or even at recess. When you've decided where you would like to approach potential friends, take a moment to listen to them and observe what they're doing. Then, think about what you would like to say. Once you have an idea about how to approach others, you'll be ready for the next step: choosing people to speak with and starting to get to know them!

Making Observations

When looking around for a potential friend, watch for clues that a person is open to speaking with you. Here are a few things to look for:

- If someone smiles in your direction, it may mean that person is open to getting to know you! Think about smiling back and even saying hello.

- If a person interacts with lots of different kids and seems accepting of others, that may be a hint that he or she is comfortable getting to know new people, including you!

- If you notice that some students in school are often alone, know that this doesn't automatically mean that they are lonely. However, it may give you a good opportunity to approach them to start a one-on-one conversation. This can be easier than breaking into an existing conversation in a larger group.

- If the person is wearing a shirt with a band or sports team on it that you also like, you know that you might have at least that in common. Try asking that person about the theme of the shirt to start up a conversation. Don't be surprised, though, if the person says the shirt was a gift or a hand-me-down, and this fellow student doesn't actually know much about the subject. At least you started the conversation!

- Pay attention to what your potential friends are saying to others (without eavesdropping). If they say something that interests you, you may have found another great way to begin a conversation or join an existing one. Think about whether that moment is the right time to say something, or if it would be better to wait until another time.

Going Slow

Once you find the person you want to get to know better, it's time to think carefully about how to start connecting. It takes time to get to know someone, and it's rare to have someone move from an acquaintance to a best friend overnight. It's important to take the time to get to know each other and to build trust. For example, knowing that a person shares your interest in collecting baseball cards may give you an idea of what to talk about. However, a true friendship

> It's important to take the time to get to know each other and to build trust.

Kamara

Kamara had a few kids who she hung out with in school, but no really close friends. Wanting to make some new friends, she thought about the kids she saw often and decided that a girl in her dance class seemed nice. Kamara was determined to become friends with Danielle.

Kamara decided to connect with Danielle at their next dance class. Any joke Danielle made in the class was met with a loud laugh from Kamara. When the dancers got ready to learn a new routine, Kamara made sure to stand right next to Danielle. At one point, Kamara even cut in between Danielle and her friend. At the end of the class, Kamara went over to Danielle and invited her to have a sleepover at her house the next weekend.

Danielle rolled her eyes and said, "I'm busy. I can't make it!" She then walked away from Kamara. Kamara was confused. She felt that she did everything in order to connect with Danielle.

- ° Can you tell what Kamara did that might have made Danielle feel uncomfortable or annoyed?
- ° What can Kamara do next to try to get to know Danielle without seeming intrusive or rushing the friendship?
- ° What would you have done differently if you wanted to get to know Danielle?

means that you understand what makes that person happy, what that person does outside of this one activity, and how that person feels about you.

If you try to rush that connection, it could feel overwhelming or confusing for both of you. Luckily, there is no time limit on making a friend. Start talking and see how that goes. If you feel comfortable, then you might want to get together in school for a project or plan an activity outside of school. Repeat, repeat, repeat. Each time you're together, you are learning about each other. Over time, this person might become your friend!

Getting Started

So how can you begin to get to know someone? Start by being yourself. Being true to yourself will show others who you are and the kind of great friend you can be. Here are a few more tips for starting a connection with a potential new friend:

- Offer a genuine compliment, without exaggeration. For example, if the person gave an interesting presentation in class, say just that. Don't exaggerate by saying something like, "That's the best presentation I've ever heard," (unless it's true!).

- Find an area of common interest and talk about it. For example, if you know the person likes basketball and you do too, ask if this potential new friend plays on a team, plays just for fun, or mostly likes watching college or professional games.

- Show an interest in the person without being intrusive. For example, on a Monday morning at school, just ask a simple question like, "How was your weekend?"

- If you are part of a group chat or on social media with the person you want to get to know, be conscious of your words and make sure you are treating others with respect. Talking negatively about someone, making fun of someone, or other similar behavior can really backfire when trying to make friends.

- Remember to listen. If you interrupt or don't really pay attention, it may lead others to get the feeling that you don't want to get to know more about them.

- If you have a friend who is also friends with someone you want to get to know, ask your friend if the three of you can hang out.

- Try to always show that you are kind and caring. These characteristics are very important to most kids when they are making new friends.

As you take these tips into consideration and try them out, remember to be yourself and take your time when becoming friends with someone new.

Getting a "No"

There may be times you ask someone to do something and they say "no." This can be painful and make you feel bad or sad. You may feel like giving up on getting to know that person. On the other hand, maybe you decide that you should keep asking until the person finally agrees to give your friendship a chance.

When kids say no when you invite them to an event, it can feel like a painful rejection. There are a few reasons someone might say no:

- A "no" may mean that someone really doesn't want to hang out with you or doesn't feel that you have anything in common.

- It may only mean "Not yet," because the person you asked may feel that the two of you really don't know each other too well. If it is a kid from school, you may want to get to know the person better in school before getting together outside of school.

Jacob

Jacob wanted to make some new friends and decided he wanted to get to know David better. During his science class with David, he noticed that David often wore sports jerseys and liked talking about sports. Jacob asked his parents if they would buy four tickets to a local baseball game. Jacob thought this would be the perfect event to attend with David. His parents agreed to buy the tickets and Jacob was hopeful that David would come to the game.

Jacob was excited to get to school the next day. When he arrived, he immediately went over to David and invited him to the game, which was two weeks away. David smiled but then said, "I can't make it. Thanks anyway."

Jacob felt rejected. He believed that he did what he could to become friends with David, and decided he wasn't going to try again. What Jacob didn't know was that David was happy to have been invited, but he truly had other plans for that date. David also felt a little uncomfortable with the idea of going to the game with Jacob and his parents when he barely knew Jacob.

° What would you have done to get to know David?
° If David said no, what would you have done then?

- The potential friend may not like the activity but would be willing to do something else.

- The other person might have believed that you were joking because the two of you haven't interacted before, so your invitation wasn't taken seriously.

There are times when people say no because they truly don't want to be friends. That may hurt your feelings. You may wonder what's wrong with you. You may withdraw and be too nervous to try again to get to know someone else. If someone clearly rejects you, here are some ways to get past it:

- Remember why you like yourself. Be a friend to yourself. Focus on the abilities, talents, and personality traits that would make you a good friend to the right person.

- Think about why you picked the other person to be friends with, and what you've now learned that may change your mind. Maybe the other person only wants to hang out with an already established close circle of friends right now. Maybe the other person felt that you rushed getting to know them. The other person may even feel uncomfortable being around someone who gets good grades, because it's not as easy for him or her. Think about whether you want to be friends with someone who rejects you. In the future, you can always rethink your decision, but for now it may be time to look for a friend who accepts you.

- It's rare for someone to become friends with everyone. If one connection didn't work, see if your approach was rushed (such as with Kamara earlier in this chapter). If not, you may want to move on and try to get to know a few other people.

- If you feel unsettled by the rejection, it's okay to take a short break from seeking friends. Spend time doing activities that you enjoy. Enjoy your own company! However, after the break, try to think about getting to know other kids again.

- If you can't get past your feelings of hurt, anger, embarrassment, or other similar emotions, you're really giving the other person too much power. That other kid truly is just one person with one reaction and one opinion. There are other possible friends waiting to meet you. Speak to an adult you trust who can help you to move past this.

Communication isn't always easy, but it's key to avoiding misunderstandings. It helps you to understand if a 'no' means 'not now but maybe later,' or if a 'no' means to look for a connection with someone else. As you develop new friendships step by step, keep an open mind, communicate with others, and remember to have fun along the way!

When to Keep Trying

If there are people you tried to make friends with who weren't interested, don't worry. In some cases, the person may have just been busy. In other cases, if the person really wasn't interested, just remember you are a valuable person and there are likely lots of people who you can make friends with who would want to be friends with you. When you're not sure, these three tips may help you figure out when to keep trying to get to know someone and when to stop:

While you are busy trying to make new friends, remember that others may also be trying to get to know you.

- If you try to talk with another kid and that kid walks away or verbally insults you, know that it's not worth trying to make friends, since you want friends who appreciate you. Take pride in your effort to become friends but find someone else who will be open to getting to know you.

- If you ask to get together with someone and they respectfully say no, wait for a few days or maybe even a few weeks, and then try again. It's possible you'll get a different response. If you try three times and hear 'no' three times, take a break. Let the other person approach you next time. If you don't hang out right away, it doesn't mean you won't be friends later on.

- Listen to feedback the other person gives you. For example, if you invite someone to play video games and they respond, "Sorry, I don't like videogames," remember that and ask to do something else next time, or ask the other person for a suggestion about what to do.

Getting to Know You

While you are busy trying to make new friends, remember that others may also be trying to get to know you. If some kids approach you in a kind and positive way, it gives you an opportunity to show who you are and also get to know them. For example, if a classmate asks you to explain a homework assignment, and you take the time to do it, you're not only helping your classmate, but you're also showing the person that you are thoughtful and caring.

Making friends can be fun and exciting. At times it may also be hard. As you go through the process, be yourself, work on feeling confident, and treat others with kindness and respect. Behaving with integrity, and being the kind of person who helps others to feel good and appreciated, can show others that you could be a valuable friend to them.

Call to Action

As you go through your day, pay attention to those around you. Can you identify one or two kids who you might get along with at school, at a sporting event, or at a club? Try to casually start a conversation with them. You can ask them about how long they have been playing the sport, tell them about an interesting activity that you did, or just have relaxed conversations about your day. You might also want to give a genuine compliment. For instance, at an art club, you may want to say, "Wow, that's a great cartoon! How did you learn to draw like that?" It may take some time and some work to connect with others, but when you develop that close group of trusted friends, it will all have been worth it!

3

BEING A GOOD FRIEND

BY NOW YOU HOPEFULLY HAVE AN IDEA OF WHAT kind of friend you're looking for and have thought about how to make friends. But have you ever thought about what kind of friend you would like to be? To attract the types of people you want as friends, it's important to show others that you have the positive qualities you look for in them.

In this chapter, you will have the opportunity to think about how you can be a trusted and caring friend. Often, great friends are kind, respectful, and do their best to be upstanders. If you haven't heard of the term 'upstander' yet, it is a person who stands up for what is right and speaks out when someone or a group is being mistreated. You'll get the chance to learn more about how to be an upstander later in this chapter.

Before we jump in, take a few minutes to answer the questions on the next page. This quiz will help you think about what kind of a friend you can be: how you show others who you are by your words and actions, how you feel about being an upstander, and how you handle being competitive with someone close to you.

Quiz

1. **As you walk to school with your friend, she slips and falls in a muddy puddle. You notice that she's very upset and she goes back home to clean up. You continue to school. Once at school, you:**

   a. tell your other friends what happened and laugh about it. They laugh too, so it must be okay to share this funny story!

   b. realize that your friend was embarrassed, so you don't tell anyone what happened.

   c. realize that your friend was embarrassed, so you keep it quiet and text your friend that you're sorry she had a rough morning.

2. **At recess, you notice that someone is being teased because of an answer he gave in math class. You also know that he is often teased and not included in activities. You:**

   a. decide that he should learn how to make some friends. You feel frustrated that he only talks with his teachers and ignores the kids at school.

   b. feel sad that he is alone and often teased. But you can't do anything about it.

   c. decide to be an upstander and tell the other students that there is no reason to tease him. You also say hello when you see him the next morning.

3. Your friend told you that he was disappointed that he didn't make the chess team. You:

a. are happy that you will have more time with this friend because he won't be at chess practice, so you ignore his feelings.

b. understand that your friend isn't happy, but you aren't sure what to do about it, so you don't respond.

c. understand that your friend isn't happy and tell him that you are there to support him. It's true that you like having time to hang out, but you didn't want him to be disappointed.

4. You know that your friend has lots of talents. At times, however, she struggles and gets frustrated when trying to work on things that are hard for her. You:

a. realize that she's good at lots of things, so you feel it's good for her to struggle sometimes.

b. want to help your friend feel better, but think if you give her a pep talk, she might get conceited, so you don't say anything.

c. don't want to see your friend upset. You share that you sometimes struggle, too. Also, you remind her about her areas of strength. You know that your friend would help you if you needed it!

5. You find out that your friend was at someone else's house on a day that she had promised to hang out with you. She apologizes and says that she forgot and didn't mean to hurt you. You:

a. end the friendship. Who wants a friend who forgets a promise?

b. aren't sure if you can still trust your friend. You decide to break a promise to her and see how she handles it.

c. really value this friend. She has never broken a promise before, and she's usually very trustworthy. You tell her that you forgive her.

Quiz Results

If you answered mostly 'a,' then you may have a hard time showing that you care about your friend when you are trying to deal with your own feelings (e.g., of being hurt).

If you answered mostly 'b,' then you are generally aware of how others might be feeling, but you may need to work on how to support your friend or classmate.

If you answered mostly 'c,' then you may already know a lot about how to be a compassionate friend and upstander! As you continue reading, you'll still get the chance to learn some important tips for being a good friend to others.

While all friendships are different, there are some common tips for being a good friend. Here are some ways to demonstrate that you can be a close and trusted friend:

- Show empathy and kindness.
- Be an upstander and discourage teasing.
- Build trust.
- Show respect to others.
- Show appreciation for your friend.
- Avoid being controlling.
- Forgive minor mistakes.
- Think about the possibility of working through big mistakes.
- Handle competition gracefully.

By practicing these positive behaviors, you can build a strong foundation of trust and connection with others. Being kind and trustworthy can help you start a good friendship or get through problems with a friend. Let's look at some of these tips in more detail.

Showing Empathy and Kindness

Empathy can simply mean that you understand someone else's feelings and perspective, even if your own feelings would be different in a similar situation. For example, if someone made a comment about your clothes looking wrinkled, you might find it funny, but some of your friends might find the same comment hurtful. If you cared about these friends, you

Being kind and trustworthy can help you start a good friendship or get through problems with a friend.

would avoid making that kind of comment to them and discourage others from doing it, too. You could also comfort your friends, if you knew their feelings were hurt.

Empathy and kindness aren't always easy. You may not always want to focus on another person's feelings. Imagine if you really want your friend to go with you to a particular movie, but you know your friend doesn't want to see it. Do you pressure your friend and focus only on your goal for the two of you to go to the movie? Take a moment to think about how you would feel if your roles were reversed, and your friend was ignoring your discomfort.

Empathy and kindness are key ingredients in developing friendships. If you show that you are a kind person who is supportive toward your friends, eventually many others may see you as both trustworthy and caring.

Be an Upstander

As mentioned above, upstanders are people who stand up for others, discourage teasing, and try to make a situation better for those around them. Upstanders try to identify situations where someone needs support, or where teasing and/or bullying is occurring, then try to figure out what to do to help. It's not always easy. It's important to remember that an upstander doesn't have to get involved directly. Sometimes it's best and most helpful to tell an adult, especially if you might get hurt if you intervene directly.

If you feel that it's safe and appropriate to intervene, here are some ways an upstander can help:

- Remain calm.
- Show respect for everyone.
- Remember that there may be two or more opinions or perspectives about a situation.

Jasper

Jasper, age 12, wanted to make the world a more caring, positive, and peaceful place. After talking with his parents about what he could do, he decided to start being an upstander at school.

On the way to school one day, he saw a few of his sixth-grade classmates throwing around a fourth-grader's backpack on the bus. Kids often made fun of this fourth grader because he was quick to get upset when someone did something wrong. Jasper had previously told his parents that this boy also tried to be "the bus police," and reported everyone who broke rules. Jasper knew that this annoyed many of the other kids.

On this day, Jasper decided to be an upstander. He caught the boy's backpack and quietly gave it back to him. The other sixth graders started to get upset with Jasper. But Jasper said, "Let's not get in trouble with the bus driver over this. He already told us to leave that kid alone." One of the other kids agreed, then another, and then the rest of the group sat down.

Jasper was happy that this worked, but he knew there was more he should do to help the fourth grader. He sat down next to him and said that kids don't like being told on for misbehaving especially when there's no real danger and the bus driver witnessed the situations already. Jasper suggested that, instead, the fourth grader can focus on starting a conversation with a younger child who seemed lonely. The boy took Jasper's advice, and he ended up becoming friendly with a few of the younger kids on the bus.

° What would you have done if you saw a younger student being picked on?
° Can you stand up for what's right while remaining calm?

- Distract the aggressor—try starting a conversation or offering to play a game.

- Hang out with the person being targeted—it's harder for someone to pick on a person who is in a group.

- Talk with an adult if you aren't sure how to help someone who is in danger or who repeatedly gets picked on.

If your friendship involves both of you caring about and accepting each other, and you enjoy spending time together, then just remember to compromise and show flexibility when needed.

There are times when it's important to tell an adult about a situation, especially if someone is being picked on, bullied, or harmed. In this situation, you would be telling for a positive reason, to help someone rather than to get someone in trouble (tattle-telling). If you decide that you need to involve an adult, try to be clear and specific, and try not to make assumptions about what might be happening. By doing this, you can be sure your information is as accurate as possible, which will help the adult to handle the situation.

You can be an upstander at school or anywhere you like. You can start a campaign to raise money for a local organization that helps others, and perhaps your friends will want to help. The kids who decide to join you may realize that they are upstanders, too! Having a common cause to focus on also helps people to get to know each other better and can be a great way to build friendships.

Build Trust and Be Respectful

Trustworthiness and respect are important qualities in a friend. How can you show other people that you have these traits?

There are many simple ways to show that you're respectful. Here are a few ideas:

- Say "please" and "thank you."
- Help others when they need it (for example, hold the door open for someone else as you walk into a restaurant, or offer a seat to someone who is standing on the bus or train).
- Be tolerant and accepting of others who are different from you.
- Don't tease others when they seem different or make mistakes.
- Listen when someone else is speaking.

Being trustworthy means that people can count on you. It may take time for you to earn trust, but it's important. Think about who you trust and what characteristics those people show that let you know you can count on them. Now, think about how you can show the same characteristics so others can trust and count on you. Here are some ways to earn trust:

- Follow through on promises. If you agree to work on a school project with another student, follow through.
- Show respect all day, every day.
- Avoid talking about people behind their backs—potential friends may feel that if you talk badly about others, you will talk badly about them too.

This probably all seems like common sense. However, even the most caring person may sometimes be tempted to be disrespectful or want to break a promise. It's helpful to know how you should behave, but you also need to be aware of how you are behaving. This awareness will help you catch and try to correct any behavior that's not respectful and trustworthy.

Avoid Being Controlling

Imagine if the only way to be accepted as a friend was by doing exactly what another person wanted you to do. Would you want to have a friendship like that? Most people want to have the freedom to be who they are, make their own decisions, and be accepted without having to think and act in a certain way that's dictated by someone else in order to keep a friendship.

If your friendship involves both of you caring about and accepting each other, and you enjoy spending time together, then just remember to compromise and show flexibility when needed. For example, if a friend decides to go ice skating one day, and you don't like ice skating, you can choose to not go, but later find a different activity the two of you can do together. Or, if you're comfortable, perhaps you try ice skating even though it's not your favorite activity. Compromising shows that you are willing to be flexible and to sometimes do activities that make the other person happy (but know that you should never compromise on something that could be potentially dangerous or harmful).

Forgiving Mistakes

We all make mistakes. Some mistakes may go unnoticed or be so minor that you can easily overlook them. Maybe a friend forgot to text you the pages for the math homework after you had asked for them. You casually text and ask for the math pages again. Your friend realizes her mistake, apologizes for not sending you the information earlier, and then sends it to you. It's not a big deal to either of you.

A big mistake may be harder to forgive. For instance, imagine if your friend planned a party on a weekend when you were going on vacation with your family. The party was important to you and you had been looking forward to it for weeks. You had told your friend the dates when you would be away, but that was a while ago. You think your friend purposely picked a time when you weren't around for the party, but you calm down and speak with him. He seems sincere when he tells you that he forgot and thought you were going away the following weekend. Can you forgive your friend?

Simone

Simone, age 10, was outgoing and had a large group of friends. One day, Simone began to feel annoyed with her friend Penny. Penny and Simone used to have a lot in common. But Penny recently started playing the violin rather than the clarinet, which is the instrument Simone plays. Penny also started playing tennis instead of continuing to play soccer with Simone.

Simone didn't directly tell Penny that she was feeling hurt and annoyed. Instead, Simone began to talk negatively about Penny to their friends. Simone made comments such as, "Penny can't run fast. That's probably why she's trying tennis now instead of playing soccer." When another friend tried to defend Penny, Simone got angry and rolled her eyes with frustration.

Soon, Simone realized that some of her friends weren't hanging out with her as much, and Penny seemed more popular than ever. All their friends seemed to be spending more time with Penny. Simone was confused and even more upset. She didn't realize that her friends were annoyed that she was being disrespectful. They felt that she was no longer trustworthy. If she turned her back on Penny, Simone's friends believed that she could turn on them too.

- ° What would you have done if your feelings were hurt because a friend started to participate in activities that didn't include you?
- ° Do you think Simone should have shared her feelings with Penny? If so, what could she have said?

Here are some ways to work toward forgiveness:

- If the mistake was truly an oversight, try to understand that. When a mistake happens, it can be easier to forgive that person when you know that it wasn't done on purpose and when you realize that your friend does respect your feelings.

- Speak in a calm, respectful, and clear way to the person who made the mistake. Then listen respectfully to the response. In the next chapter, you will learn ways to do this.

- If the person felt the mistake was minor, but you disagree, tell the other person how it made you feel. Maybe sharing your feelings will help your friend to better understand you and have more compassion. Just make sure that you don't sound accusatory.

- Speak with a parent or another trusted adult for advice about whether it's okay to forgive your friend. If you would rather speak with another friend, think carefully about what you say so it doesn't seem like you're talking badly about the person who hurt your feelings.

- If you are generally happy having this person in your life, work toward getting past the mistake. Focus on what you enjoy about the friendship and share this with the other person. Then, calmly and respectfully ask if the two of you can talk about how to move forward. Find a time when you both can focus on talking without rushing somewhere and without an audience of other kids around. You or your friend may come up with a great solution!

Remembering that everyone makes mistakes can help you to forgive others. You probably would want to be forgiven too. There is a big difference between someone making a mistake and someone trying to hurt you. When a mistake is made, or a disagreement happens, getting past it in a positive way can improve your friendship and help it grow. Tips on positive ways to resolve disagreements are highlighted in Chapter 4.

Handling Competition

Competition can be a good thing. It can motivate people to work hard and be the best they can be in a particular field or activity, such as sports, baking, math, or spelling. Sometimes being in a competition can also be a challenge: if you are competing with a friend and you both really want to win, it may be hard to be supportive of each other. How do you cheer on your friend while also doing your best to win? And what do you do if you win or if you lose? Here are some tips on how to be a fair and polite competitor either way:

- Be kind and respectful to each other during competitions.
- Know that it's okay to try your hardest and to win, even if your friend is disappointed from the loss. The key is to be there to support and encourage your friend, no matter who's winning.
- It's also okay for your friend to try really hard to win, even if it means that you lose!
- Be a thoughtful winner. Don't gloat or show off. It's important to show that you're sensitive to your friend's feelings.
- On a similar note, be a thoughtful competitor even when you don't win. Don't show anger or envy if your friend wins. Remember that you both worked hard.
- Remember that you care about each other and are friends first and competitors second.

If you are a winner, it's easy to be happy and excitedly tell everyone you won. But try to think about your friend and her feelings. On the other hand, if you don't win and your friend does, it's okay to feel sad, disappointed, and even a little frustrated. No feeling is wrong or bad. How you react, though, can affect a friendship. It's not always easy to support and compliment a friend after competing against each other. It's important, though, to recognize the win and say congratulations. This is a way of being not just a competitor and a team player, but also a thoughtful friend. Then, try sharing your frustration with your parents or other trusted adults, because it can help to speak up about your feelings. Hopefully, this can help you feel better about the situation and stay supportive of your friend's win. Isn't this what you would hope your friend would do for you, if you had won? Once you've taken some time to process and feel better about not winning, maybe you and your friend can teach each other some techniques so you can both gain more skills!

Call to Action

When was the last time that you complimented a friend? Most people feel appreciated and supported when another person acknowledges their abilities or special qualities. Think about a few of your friends. Can you come up with an ability or a skill that they each have? Perhaps you notice they are great at math when you're doing homework together. Maybe they shared some amazing sketches with you. Give specific, clear, and genuine compliments without expecting one back. Complimenting another person's strengths shows that you're a caring friend and helps that person to feel appreciated by you.

4

SURVIVING DISAGREEMENTS

MINOR DISAGREEMENTS, AND EVEN INTENSE ARGUMENTS, sometimes happen between friends. If you and a friend have a conflict, feelings may get hurt and it may feel like your friendship will end. Knowing how to cope with these stressful situations is important. Why? Because if a conflict comes up, you will know how to deal with it. It can be hard, but there are ways to handle conflicts and even sometimes become better friends after getting through them.

In this chapter, you will learn about respectful problem-solving and how to work through conflicts. These skills can make the difference between keeping a friend or losing one.

Before getting started, take the quiz on the next page. It will help you think about how you handle conflict. There are no wrong answers. However, these questions can help you to think about whether you have the tools to deal with conflicts or if more information would help you to feel better prepared to handle disagreements.

Quiz

1. **You and your good friend usually play basketball at recess. Recently, your friend has started sitting on the bench instead, just talking with you and the other kids. Do you:**

    a. say to your friend, "Stop just sitting there. What's wrong with you?"

    b. talk with your friend while he is on the bench, but admit that it's not your favorite recess activity? You would rather do something else.

    c. tell your friend that you'll sometimes stay on the bench to talk, but on most days, you would prefer to play basketball and hope that you can still sometimes play together?

2. **You found out that your best friend invited another friend to the planetarium. You felt excluded. So you:**

    a. decide not to invite her to your upcoming birthday party. You want her to feel as excluded as you felt.

    b. text this friend and let her know that she hurt your feelings, but you don't respond when she texts back. You aren't sure how to work through the conflict.

    c. talk to your friend. You say that you were disappointed that she didn't invite you to go. Then you listen to what she says and try to see if there is a way to resolve the conflict.

3. You are surprised when your friend laughs and says, "Your computer project was so nerdy. Congratulations!" You:

   a. assume your friend was making fun of you. You later laugh at him and say, "I can't believe you didn't get a 100 on that test."

   b. realize that you have no idea what your friend meant and you don't know how to ask. You pretend that your friend never made that statement so you can keep being friends.

   c. find time to talk with your friend. You are relieved to learn that he meant "nerdy" in the same way others might say "smart!"

4. A friend lets you know that another close friend, Nina, is mad because you were laughing with a kid in class and wouldn't tell her what was so funny. Knowing this information, you:

   a. get angry that Nina needs to know everything. You then purposely talk and laugh with other kids to teach this 'friend' that you aren't going to share everything with her.

   b. tell Nina that you weren't laughing at her. After that, you don't feel like you need to do anything else to help your friend feel better.

   c. speak with Nina. You listen to why she was mad and try to resolve the problem together.

5. Your friend is at your home when you and your parents get into a disagreement. While your parents talk calmly, you get really angry and yell at them and slam your bedroom door. Turning toward your friend, you say, "Aren't my parents mean?" Your friend says you might have over-reacted. You:

a. tell your friend that's totally wrong and stop hanging out.

b. tell your friend that you don't think so, but that you understand how it looked. You try to calm down and enjoy your time together.

c. acknowledge your friend's view and say that you'll think about it. You feel that being honest is an important part of a friendship and you are happy they trusted you enough to be honest.

Quiz Results

If you answered mostly 'a,' then you may be struggling to find a way to work through conflicts with friends. There are lots of helpful tips in this chapter!

If you answered mostly 'b,' then you already have an idea about how to problem-solve when you have a disagreement with someone else, but you still have some

questions about how to do it well.
If you answered mostly 'c,' then you already know a lot about how to respectfully resolve disagreements. As you continue reading, though, you may pick up some new tips!

Should You Talk It Out?

You may have been told that it's always good to share your feelings and talk things out. This is usually great advice! There are a few times, though, when it's better not to say anything.

Imagine if you felt embarrassed by the way one friend moved her hands when she talked and the way another friend dressed. Should you tell them how you feel? Sometimes sharing opinions or reactions like this can end up insulting your friends. For this reason, it's important to think before you speak.

When deciding whether to share your discomfort with your friend, consider these three points:

- Is the issue important to discuss because you're being hurt by it (for example, you have a friend who thinks it's funny to smack you in the back of the head to say hello)?

- Is the issue affecting your friendship (for example, your friend suddenly stopped hanging out with you during recess, and you don't know why)?

- Is your friend mistreating someone else and you want to be an upstander, but you also want to stay friends?

If the answer to any of these questions is "yes," you have good reasons to talk things out. However, if you're trying to change some things about friends that they can't control or they enjoy, such as the way they walk, or something to do with their personal preferences, such as how they dress, or a hobby they enjoy that you don't like to do, your friends will probably not take it well. It's important to understand that your friends are always going to be different from you in some ways. That doesn't mean they're wrong. It just means everyone is unique, and accepting differences is a key part of making and keeping friends!

Talking It Out

When you're having a conflict with a friend that you would like to talk through, there are some things you can do to increase the chances of working things out. Before starting a conversation, though, think about you and your friend. Are both of you comfortable and open to talking through problems? If not, it might be helpful to ask a trusted adult for advice on how to become more comfortable, or how to help your friend to be more comfortable. Then you can begin to talk through your issues. Here are some points to consider when having the conversation:

- Does your friend agree that there is a conflict? If not, calmly let your friend know that you are uncomfortable and want to talk something out. Try not to get angry or frustrated that your friend didn't notice the problem. Sometimes friends may not notice the same things in a friendship.

- If you and your friend agree that you need to talk, find a time when you won't have to rush. You will need enough time to both talk and listen to the other person's thoughts. Otherwise, you may not have time to fully understand each other's perspective and resolve the issue.

- Talk in private if you can. If other people are around, they may try to take sides or add their own viewpoints, which can be distracting and change the focus of your conversation.

When it comes time to have a conversation, you or your friend may be nervous. That's okay. You can each help the conversation go smoothly by keeping the tone of the talk calm and respectful. It may also be helpful to agree to some rules, such as avoiding accusations and not interrupting when the other person is speaking.

Sasha

Sasha, age 12, was hurt and angry when she heard from Anne that one of her best friends, Tanya, was making fun of how Sasha played soccer in gym class. Sasha thanked Anne for telling her and then avoided Tanya because she was so hurt.

After confiding in her parents, Sasha decided to talk things out with Tanya. She wanted to end the friendship or make fun of Tanya to other kids, but her parents told her that she should try to resolve the conflict and should never act in a hurtful way. After thinking about her parents' comments, Sasha agreed with them and realized that she didn't want to be known as a kid who purposely upsets anyone.

Sasha texted Tanya the next morning and asked to meet at school before class. When she saw Tanya, Sasha remembered her parents' advice. She stayed calm and respectful and remembered not to assume that Tanya meant to hurt her. She said, "I heard about something that you may have done, and it hurt my feelings. Can we talk later?"

Tanya seemed totally confused but said okay. They got together after school, so they could speak in private. When Tanya heard what Anne had told Sasha, Tanya didn't deny what happened. She started to cry and said, "I was making fun of a lot of kids, including myself, about how we can't play soccer. What was I thinking? I'm so sorry!"

Sasha had a choice to accept the apology or not. She felt that Tanya was sincere and after Tanya apologized, promised never to do this again, and said that she didn't mean to hurt Sasha, the two hugged and the problem was solved!

- ° If you were in Sasha's position, would you have talked things out with Tanya?
- ° If you were Tanya, could you admit your mistake and work to correct it?
- ° If you were Anne, would you have told Sasha what happened?

It can be difficult to remain calm when your feelings are hurt and you are angry at your friend. When you're feeling emotional, it's possible that the rules you agreed to follow won't be easy to stick to and your conversation could get heated. You both may want to shout or say things to hurt the other. In this situation, it's best to stop and find another time to talk. Doing this will give each of you time to calm down and think about your friendship. Later, you can come together to try again if you both agree to do so.

If you feel that you might need help to calm down, try some of these strategies:

- Breathe in slowly through your nose, hold it for three seconds, and breathe out slowly through your mouth. Do this three or four times.

- Think of a calming image such as a favorite vacation spot. Hold on to it in your mind.

- Tighten and then relax your muscles, starting with your forehead and working your way down your body until you tighten and then relax your toes. Spend 1-2 seconds tensing and 1-2 seconds relaxing each muscle group before moving to another area to relax. Be gentle. Don't tighten to the point where it feels uncomfortable or painful. Focusing on this process can help you to relax and reduce the tension in your body.

- Remind yourself that yelling may decrease your chances of being understood.

- Think of how you want to be treated and try to treat your friend that way.

- Do something that brings you happiness and relaxation before you talk with your friend. Exercise, listen to music, or read a great book.

- Ask a trusted adult for other solutions.

If you and your friend can be calm and respectful, chances are that you will be better able to listen to each other and think about ways to work through your disagreement.

When you and your friend are ready to start talking, try following these steps:

If you and your friend can be calm and respectful, chances are that you will be better able to listen to each other and think about ways to work through your disagreement.

1. Decide who will speak first: remember that if both of you are talking at the same time, it may be difficult for either of you to really listen to the other.

2. After that person speaks, the other person should restate what was heard. This is important since sometimes people hear one thing when the speaker meant something different.

3. If the listener misunderstood something that the speaker said, then the speaker should clarify his or her meaning.

4. Next, let the second person speak and repeat steps (2) and (3).

5. As each of you speaks, respectfully clarify what you believe happened and what your intentions were. For example: "I wasn't trying to ignore you. I was just trying to find a way to get to know the new person and you weren't around when I went to hang out with him." The second person may say in response, "I thought you just wanted to hang out with the new kid, so I walked away." This helps clarify the conflict as a misunderstanding.

6. Rather than accusing your friend of something, focus on how you perceived the situation, how it made you feel, and your desire to resolve things. You can try something called 'I' messages. Here is a basic 'I' message:

   I felt _____ when _____ because _____. I want _____.

If you start talking by saying "You shouldn't have..." the sentence may seem accusatory. The first speaker in step 5 could use an "I" message like this one: "I felt ignored and hurt when you started hanging out with that new kid because I felt left out. I want to hang out like we used to do all the time." This is a clear statement that doesn't verbally attack the friend.

7. Keep in mind that it's sometimes a sign of strength to apologize. If you did something that you wish you hadn't done, it shows strong character to admit it and promise to be more careful in the future. If you feel that you didn't do anything wrong, you can still apologize for unintentionally upsetting your friend. This may help you work together to find a way to resolve the problem.

Finding a Solution

There may be times when you feel strongly about ending a friendship with someone who is behaving in ways that you disagree with, such as teasing others. But first you may want to try to convince your friend to stop this behavior. Keep in mind your friend might not have realized that an action was mean or hurtful. In this case, talk with your friend honestly about how you feel and see how your friend reacts. If you try to resolve an issue before giving up on a friendship, you may find that you still have a great friend and can work through the difficulty. One day the situation may be reversed. A friend may be uncomfortable with something you did, and you may not have realized you did anything wrong. Wouldn't you want to have a chance to think about your friend's discomfort and consider ways that you might work through the situation?

Rather than accusing your friend of something, focus on how you perceived the situation, how it made you feel, and your desire to resolve things.

Ken and Owen

Ken and Owen did almost everything together. They played the same sports, hung out with the same kids, and even did class projects together. When Ken told Owen that he was excited that his parents signed him up for art classes, Owen was upset. He didn't like art and tried to convince Ken to sign up for ice hockey lessons with him instead.

Ken listened respectfully to his friend's reasons, then gave his own reasons for wanting to take art lessons. They tried to compromise. Ken said that he'll do the art class now and maybe take ice hockey lessons next year. This didn't satisfy Owen.

Eventually, these close friends agreed that they enjoyed their friendship too much to let this issue separate them. They agreed to accept the fact that they will have some different experiences and it wasn't a rejection of the other person. Ken and Owen both ended up enjoying hearing about each other's lessons.

° If either boy had demanded that the other join his activity, what do you think might have happened to their friendship?
° What would you do if you and your friend were in a similar situation?

Keep in mind that it's sometimes a sign of strength to apologize.

Sometimes disagreements are easy to work through. Each person shares their feelings and thoughts, then they agree that there was a misunderstanding and apologize! Sometimes, though, it's not so easy. In either case, you can start by trying to communicate with your friend and try your best to solve the problem. Negotiating and compromising with your friend may also help.

At times, you and your friend might want to compromise in order to resolve a conflict. You may not get everything you want, and your friend may not either. However, both of you may get enough to feel comfortable and satisfied. For example, perhaps you and your friend agree to have at least one sleepover each month with just the two of you, and then you agree to sometimes hang out with your friend in groups.

When trying to resolve conflicts, you have to decide how strongly you feel about an issue and how flexible you can be. Is something bothering you so much that you are willing to lose your friend over it? Or is there a way to come to an agreement and stay friends? Being flexible, respectful, and finding ways to compromise may help you to have an even stronger friendship after the issue is resolved!

When You Can't Agree

It's often comforting to know that you and a friend both understand that a problem exists and want to work to resolve it. However, if you feel there's a conflict and your friend does not, sometimes it's okay just to share your feelings and thank your friend for listening. Later, your friend may or may not realize that you were right. Or, you may realize that you misunderstood your friend's actions.

Calling a truce over a disagreement, even if you can't resolve it, can sometimes be helpful. You may consider calling a truce if you don't think the issue is a major problem and you do feel that the friendship is otherwise good. If both of you want to start over, calling a truce might be all that's needed to resolve the problem and stay friends.

It's also okay to disagree but decide to move on, depending on the situation. Think about whether you should get an apology, or if your priority is to move past the problem and save the friendship. If you are comfortable moving past the problem, have a talk about the issue with your friend. Hopefully, both of you will agree that you don't want this problem to come up again. Many people would prefer an apology but can accept a promise that both people will work hard to do better in the future.

People have different interests and values. Someone's feelings may have been so hurt that staying friends seems impossible. For example, imagine that you know for sure that your friend has been rolling her eyes when you talk and has started being rude to you or ignoring you at school. When you try to talk, she has no interest in listening. What should you do?

Here are some things you can try if something like this happens:

- Try taking a friendship break. It's possible you may end up being friends again later.

- Be respectful. You may be tempted to tell other kids why you two aren't friends anymore and convince the others to take your side. Try to avoid talking negatively about your former friend, though, as this could make things more hurtful.

- Avoid asking other friends to get involved. For example, don't ask others to choose you as a friend over the other person. Think about how that might make someone feel.

- Speak with a trusted adult. Ending a friendship can be a big loss. Before you follow through with it, try to get the advice of someone you trust.

As you move forward, if you aren't sure that you trust your friend, or your feelings were hurt because of that person's actions, be careful not to consider this former friend as an enemy now. You may want to move that person into the acquaintance category in your circle of friendship and trust (see Chapter 1). Then, see if you want to work on developing a friendship again later, even if it's slightly different than the one you just ended. If you have tried everything to resolve a problem with a friend and you no longer speak, don't keep your feelings in. Talk to a parent or other trusted adult. It can be hard to lose a friend. Take time to process the situation and then refocus on the future and your social life without that friend, for now.

Handling Sadness, Hurt, and Anger

If you feel that a friend betrayed or hurt you, it may be hard to move past it. Even if you try to talk it out with your friend, your friend may not admit to the action or may not apologize. If your friend does apologize, you may still have feelings of sadness, hurt, or anger.

What can you do if you are still upset after you work out an issue with a friend or if you decide to take a break from the friendship? Here are some tips:

- Think about whether you need to do anything else to fix the situation (for example, do you need to apologize? Do you need to try to compromise?).

- Use self-talk, which basically means you talk to yourself about something. You can tell yourself that you are proud of how you handled the situation, even though it didn't end up the way you wanted. This can help you feel a bit better. Self-talk is also about reminding yourself that you are a worthwhile person and can either learn from your mistake or move past the pain because you have new adventures awaiting!

- Use calming techniques and mindfulness, such as imagining yourself on a relaxing vacation, or take calming deep breaths.

- Be careful not to accidentally (or purposely) try to get back at another person. Revenge can be harmful to your friend, but also to you. It's not a healthy way to respond to conflict and it can hurt your reputation!

- Keep busy. Get involved in activities you enjoy and hang out with other kids. Laugh and have fun!

If you keep trying to move past the conflict, but you find that you're still upset, it's definitely time to talk with trusted adults. Do you have a few adults in your life who you feel comfortable talking with about your problems? There are also experts, who can help you process your thoughts and feelings. Reach out by letting your parent know you need to talk, seek out the school guidance counselor or school psychologist, or ask your parent or guidance counselor to set up an appointment for you to talk to someone else who is an expert on helping kids with social challenges.

Call to Action

Next time you're watching a TV show about kids hanging out together, or even just watching how kids at school interact, notice when a conflict comes up and try to think of how you would handle a similar situation. It's sometimes easier to come up with solutions when you aren't directly involved and feeling emotional. Hold on to your solution if you think it's a good one. Maybe you will need to follow your own advice one day! If you aren't sure how to handle the conflicts you witness, try brainstorming with a trusted adult to come up with a plan you could use if you are ever having a similar disagreement.

5

BEST FRIENDS

DO YOU HAVE A BEST FRIEND? IF YOU DON'T HAVE one, would you like to have one? If the answer is yes, have you thought about why? Some kids prefer to have lots of very good friends but no best friend. Others definitely want a best friend. There are some kids who have had the same best friend for many years, while others change best friends frequently. In this chapter, you will have the opportunity to think about your relationship with your best friend, if you have one, or what it would mean to have a best friend, if you don't. It can be wonderful to have that special, close friend, but it's not always easy to stay best friends as you both change over time.

Before reading about best friends, take a few minutes to answer the questions on the next page. The goal is for these questions to help you think about what kind of person you want as a best friend, how to work to get a best friend, and how you would handle conflicts.

Quiz

1. **When you think about what kind of best friend you want, you:**

   a. want a best friend who listens to everything you say, does what you want, and only hangs out with you.

   b. want a best friend who likes to hang out with you, but you aren't sure how you will feel if that best friend has other good friends too.

   c. know that you want to have that one special friend, but you also want other friends.

2. **You know that sharing time with a person who is trustworthy, fun, and really understands you would make you happy. You get along well with a teammate on your soccer team. You want to be his best friend, so you:**

   a. tell him bad things about his other friends, in the hopes that he will stop hanging out with them and become your best friend.

   b. hang out with this person all the time in a group setting with other teammates, but you're not sure how to become closer friends.

   c. hang out at soccer practice, and after getting to know him better, you begin hanging out, off the field. You understand that it can take time for a close friendship to develop.

3. **You enjoy your best friend, but sometimes get frustrated when she wants to be your only friend. You want this best friendship to be fun and flexible. One day, your parents get tickets to see a musical and tell you that you can invite two friends. You know that your best friend won't be happy if you invite someone else too. You:**

   a. feel like this is a special event and your best friend needs to deal with the fact that you are inviting someone else too.

   b. care about your best friend and let her know that you hope that she can have fun with you and your other friend.

   c. respectfully talk with your friend about how it's uncomfortable for you when she wants to control who you hang out with, and that you do want to spend time with other friends. You let her know you want to stay close and you hope she comes to the musical.

4. **You want a best friend who spends lots of time socializing with you. When your best friend was spending summer vacation out of town, she promised to touch base with you every day on social media. She ended up only connecting with you once a week. Your feelings are hurt. You:**

   a. hurt her back by ignoring her when she returns to town.

   b. wait for your friend to come home, then ask her why she didn't contact you every day. You hear her explanation but are more focused on your own feelings.

   c. share your feelings with your friend when she gets back home and listen to what she has to say. You both find a way to move forward with your close friendship.

5. **You were told that your best friend is spreading rumors about you to keep you from having other friends. You:**

a. start spreading rumors about him too.

b. aren't sure that you can trust this friend anymore. You want to talk about it with him, but you aren't sure what to say.

c. know you have to have a conversation to clear things up. You value the friendship and want to give your best friend a chance to tell you the truth. You also want to stop the rumors about you.

Quiz Results

If you answered mostly 'a,' then beginning or keeping up a best friendship might be difficult for you right now.

If you answered mostly 'b,' then you are generally aware of your feelings and those of your friend, but you may not be sure how to grow or keep a best friendship over time.

If you answered mostly 'c,' then you already know a lot about how to make and keep a best friend. Continue reading to learn more about being a best friend and having a best friend.

Becoming Best Friends

For some kids, having a best friend is really important. They want to have one person they can confide in and count on to spend lots of time with, talking, laughing, and doing fun activities together. Sometimes a best friendship comes together quickly, but it's more likely to take some time as you get to know and trust each other.

There are different kinds of best friendships. Some best friends are very happy hanging out mostly with each other. There are best friends who are comfortable spending time together, but also like being with other friends. Sometimes a person has several best friends. There is no wrong way to be best friends if everyone is happy and feels good about their friendships. However, later in the chapter you'll have a chance to consider a few downsides of spending all your time with just one friend.

> *Sometimes a best friendship comes together quickly, but it's more likely to take some time as you get to know and trust each other.*

Before you become best friends with someone, it's a good idea to make sure you and your best friend have the same expectations of your friendship in order to avoid problems. For example, find out how much time your best friend would want to spend with you, and how much time that person would want to spend hanging out in groups or with other kids. If you find that you each want different things, it might be better to remain good friends and enjoy your friendship without the pressure of being best friends.

As mentioned earlier, it may also take time to find and become best friends with someone. It takes time to get to know a person, to be friends with that person first, and then to be close enough that you and the other person agree to be best friends.

Here are a few things to keep in mind as you work to become best friends:

- A total stranger probably can't earn your trust instantly, even if you find that you enjoy hanging out with this new person. Think back to the circles of trust you read about in Chapter 1. You may get to know someone, get to enjoy and trust each other, and then that person could eventually move into the small, inner circle of those people who you trust most.

- What kind of person are you seeking to be your best friend? Is it a person who enjoys the same activities as you, even if you don't talk to each other much? Is it someone who you trust to share your private thoughts with, or to help you to feel better when you are down?

- Focus on being friends first. There is no exact timeframe for becoming best friends. Ask yourself if you and your friend enjoy spending lots of time together. Are you learning to trust each other?

It's important to know what you are looking for in this special friendship, even though the answers will be different for everyone. There's no need to rush the process.

Best Friend Rules

Friendships should usually be fun and rewarding. The special relationships you have with your best friends should make you feel good and supported. In these relationships, you probably don't want to hold a formal meeting about your expectations for being best friends. After all, friendship is not a business deal! However, it might be a good idea to make sure that you both share an understanding of what it means to be a best friend. A simple conversation can help avoid conflicts and hurt feelings later.

Rochelle and Vicky

Rochelle and Vicky had different expectations of each other when they became best friends. Rochelle was excited to have Vicky as her new best friend. She thought they would share secrets, spend almost all their free time together, and never hang out with other friends without each other. Vicky was also excited when she and Rochelle first became best friends. She thought it would be fun to spend time together and hang out with Rochelle and their other friends. Vicky also wanted to share stories with Rochelle about her time spent with other friends.

A few weeks after becoming best friends, Rochelle was hurt and angry with Vicky because Vicky invited her old camp friends over for a sleepover and didn't include Rochelle. Vicky was surprised and annoyed when Rochelle told her she was a bad best friend for not inviting her to the sleepover. Vicky told Rochelle that she could invite whoever she wants. The two girls decided that they would no longer be best friends, and maybe not friends at all anymore.

- ° How would you have felt if you were Rochelle or Vicky?
- ° If both girls had talked about their expectations for their friendship from the beginning, do you think this conflict could have been avoided?
- ° How do you think Rochelle or Vicky should have handled this situation?

If you and your potential new best friend talk about your expectations and both decide that you want to spend most of your free time with each other, this may just reflect how much you enjoy each other's company. That's great! However, there are a few things to think about:

- Do you want to stop or limit the time you spend hanging out with other kids?
- Do you want to limit your chances of becoming friends with other people?
- Would you feel like you were betraying your best friend if you sometimes went to activities or parties separately?
- Could you accidentally hurt other kids' feelings because they think that you and your best friend aren't interested in getting to know them?

Your best friend doesn't have to be your only friend. It can be fun to be friends with a variety of people. Having different friends can open your eyes to new adventures, cultures, activities, and much more. And you can still spend time with, and confide in, your closest friends.

Loyalty

Loyalty is an important part of friendship. What exactly is loyalty? Being loyal means that you show support for someone, that you don't talk negatively about that person to others, and that you can be consistent and trustworthy. It's important to be a loyal friend. It shows that you are caring, respectful, and dependable. This doesn't mean you should support or side with friends if what they are doing is wrong or makes you uncomfortable, though.

Juan

Juan was very outgoing. He liked to be involved in a variety of activities, and he was always interested in getting to know others. One day, Juan noticed that Andrew, one of the other students in his science class, seemed upset. As they left class, Juan casually asked Andrew if he was okay.

Andrew shook his head yes but then admitted, "My mom is really sick. She might die." Andrew was surprised that those words just came out of his mouth. He didn't mean to say anything about his mom, and asked Juan not to tell anyone. Juan promised Andrew he would keep the information private. He also let Andrew know that he was there to support him.

Juan talked to his parents that night about Andrew's serious family situation. He felt he wasn't breaking his promise by telling adults. However, Juan didn't tell his best friend, Connor. When Connor noticed that Juan and Andrew were hanging out more at school, he felt jealous. He didn't understand what had changed. Juan didn't feel comfortable telling Connor about Andrew's private family situation. Juan and Connor got into an argument, but Juan knew he just couldn't say anything about Andrew, because it wouldn't be right. After the argument, Juan's and Connor's best friendship was at risk.

- ° How would you have handled this situation with Connor if you were Juan?
- ° If you were Connor, and you knew that you were feeling jealous, how would you have handled it?

> *Your best friend doesn't have to be your only friend. It can be fun to be friends with a variety of people.*

In a friendship, sometimes you may feel that your friend wasn't loyal because you were left out of an activity or weren't told something personal that was shared with others. For instance, imagine if you found out that a classmate was moving. You tell your best friend, only to find out he knew about this for weeks but was sworn to secrecy. How would you feel? Would you appreciate the fact that your best friend respected the other student's wish to keep the information private, or would you feel that your best friend wasn't loyal to you because he didn't share the information with you?

If you find yourself in a similar situation, it's important to really think about what happened. Would you want your best friend to tell you everything about someone else, even if it's something private or personal? Though you are best friends, that shouldn't mean either of you should ignore the feelings or requests of others. The exception to this is if someone is in danger. In that case, it's important to tell a trusted adult in order to keep a friend safe. Safety needs to come first!

More Than One Best Friend

Is it possible to have more than one best friend? The answer is yes... sometimes! You may have a best friend in each situation in which you spend time: one from camp, another from your soccer team, and maybe even a best friend from when you were younger. Would you be okay if a best friend of yours also had other best friends? If not, what could you do about it? Should you ask your new best friend not to be best friends with others? Do you learn to accept the multiple best friends? Do you prefer to continue your friendship and also find another best friend who has similar expectations?

If you enjoy your friendship with your best friend and you would miss it if it ended, then maybe you can accept the fact that the other person has several best friends. If you are okay with having just some time alone with your best friend, then you might not care if the other person has other best friends. You may still be satisfied with your friendship as it is.

If you need another person to commit to only having you as a best friend, and you both are comfortable with that, then that's probably going to work out. However, if you want only one best friend and the other person wants several, then you may be headed for some trouble. Imagine if you told your best friend to stop being friends with others. You would likely get a negative reaction.

Here are some ways to feel better about having a best friend who is very close with others:

- Focus on the positive things about your friendship. Think about what you have in common with this person, rather than what you don't.

- Think about the fact that you might want to hang out with your other friends while your best friend is with hers.

- Think about why you might not feel comfortable sharing your best friend. Do you generally struggle with jealousy or the fear of being left out? If so, it might be time to get support from a trusted adult so that you feel more comfortable sharing friends.

Friends often share activities and other interests together, and make each other feel supported, cared about, and happy. If you realize that you are sensitive to situations where you feel left out, then a friendship (whether it's a best friendship or other forms of friendship) might be stressful for you. While you can't expect friends to always change so that you are comfortable, they should sometimes. For example, if a friend hurts your feelings by making a joke about you, you can want and even expect that behavior to change after you have a chance to talk about the situation in private. However, if you want your best friend to significantly change the way he or she acts, or you want to say who your best friend can spend time with, the friendship may not work out. Why? Because most people want to have freedom to behave and socialize in ways that make them comfortable and happy, too.

Handling Conflicts With Your Best Friend

Having a best friend can be an amazing experience! You can become so close that it feels like you are part of each other's family. However, just like with siblings, being really close may sometimes mean that you have to work out conflicts.

If you have a conflict with your best friend (or close friend):

- Think about whether your expectations are fair to your friend.

- Think about whether your friend's expectations of you seem fair.

- Ask for guidance from an adult if you realize that your expectations aren't fair to your friend (e.g., you don't want your best friend to have other friends).

- Consider whether there is a way to compromise, so that both of you get some of what you want (e.g., one person wants to go to an amusement park on the weekend and the other person wants to see a new movie).

- Avoid accusations. Instead, stick to sharing your thoughts and feelings and what you are hoping to resolve in the relationship.

- Remember why you became best friends in the first place. Then, show your friend respect, use a calm voice, and be flexible when you can.

Your relationship with a parent or sibling might have some ups and downs. This is also true for many friendships, even best friendships. If you and your best friend have an issue that you think you can resolve, give it a try. After all, you chose each other to be best friends for a reason. If you and your best friend get into a situation where it's clear you need help, make sure you reach out to get it. Seeking support can be a sign of courage and a strong desire to work through the issue. If a best friend tries to change you or dares you to do things that are dangerous, or you both realize that you have grown apart and don't know how to handle it, ask for help. Maybe you can completely resolve the disagreement or conflict, or even if you can't totally work it out, perhaps you can still be friends, even if your friendship becomes a little less intense for a while.

Friends often share activities and other interests together, and make each other feel supported, cared about, and happy.

If you do take a break from being best friends, it's important for both of you to continue to respect each other and honor each other's personal information that was shared when you were more comfortable together. For example, don't share who your friend has a crush on. You don't want to betray the trust you built, even if your feelings are hurt. As you read earlier, the exception to this rule is if someone is in danger or there is a serious concern. In these situations, talk to a trusted adult to make sure that everyone involved is safe.

Should Everyone Have a Best Friend?

Many happy people don't have best friends. And that's okay! They may have many friends who accept and care for them. You don't always need a best friend. But if having a close connection with one particular person makes you happy, that's okay, too! You should do whatever works for you and your friend and makes you both comfortable. If you don't have a best friend now, and you would like one, maybe you will make one in the future. Whatever your friendship situation is, make sure you're happy and that you and the other person both accept the unspoken 'rules' of the friendship. The most important thing is to have friendships that work for everyone involved and make you and your friends feel good.

Call to Action

Take some time to think about whether you want to have one best friend or if you are happy with many good friends. Remind yourself that people can be happy either way. If you want a best friend, think about why, and what your expectations are. Then see if there is someone you know who has similar expectations for having a best friend. If your expectations are different, try being good friends for now and see how that goes. If your expectations are similar, suggest a time to hang out, but don't feel the need to rush anything. Remember that becoming true best friends can take time.

6

FRIENDSHIPS AND PEER PRESSURE

HAVE YOUR FRIENDS EVER PRESSURED YOU TO DO OR say something in order to fit in? This is called peer pressure, and it can even happen to adults. Negative peer pressure can make someone believe that the only way to keep friends or be accepted is to do what others want, even if it's risky, wrong, or feels uncomfortable. But peer pressure isn't always negative. Positive peer pressure can lead a person to try new experiences that are safe, exciting, and fun.

In this chapter, you will read about the power friends can have in forming a 'group voice.' This is when all the friends in a group are expected to accept the opinion expressed by one or two leaders. The group voice can pressure someone to act in a certain way, whether it's positive or negative.

Before we dig deeper into discussing peer pressure, take a few minutes to answer the questions on the next page. They give you a chance to think about how you contribute to or respond to peer pressure. If you know how peer pressure affects you, you can more easily find tools to cope with it and know when to use them.

Quiz

1. **Your friends all decide to sign up for a fencing class. You're not interested and would rather do something else. So, you:**

   a. decide not to sign up for the lessons. When a friend asks you why you didn't show up, you say, "Oops! I forgot."

   b. sign up for tennis lessons (which you actually want to attend) that are at the same time, so you can't do both.

   c. let them know how you feel. You hope that your true friends won't mind that you don't want to join them in this particular activity.

2. **Two of your friends keep teasing you about always following the rules. Your friends then tell you they're going to tell their parents that they are sick in order to skip school and play video games. They dare you to tell your parents the same thing and join them. Do you:**

   a. agree to do this? You don't want to lose these popular friends.

   b. make a joke about how it's cool to do the right thing?

   c. talk with your friends about how you want to be accepted for who you are, including your focus on following rules?

3. **You're really happy to be in the popular group. However, the kids in this group exclude and make fun of certain kids in your grade. Do you:**

   a. avoid those excluded kids as well, since you don't want to be made fun of or kicked out of the popular group?

   b. say hello to the other kids, or get together with them outside of school, but ignore them when you are with the popular kids?

c. hang out with the popular kids, but calmly explain that you don't want to insult anyone? You try to be an upstander and communicate respect for everyone without insulting your friends.

4. **Your close friends keep pressuring you to try out for the debate team. They know that you are really good at research, respectfully giving your opinions, and debating. They feel that they are being supportive and encouraging, but you don't want to be on the team. You just like to debate others for fun. You:**

   a. get mad at these friends and say that if they continue to talk about you joining the debate team you won't be friends anymore.

   b. tell them that you can't join because you're busy on the days when the team meets. This isn't true, but it stops your friends from annoying you.

   c. have an honest conversation with your friends. You thank them for believing in you but tell them that you're feeling uncomfortable with how often they ask you to try out, because you don't want to.

5. **Your friends all agree that everyone should tell their parents they are going to Joseph's house to hang out. Joseph's parents are out of town, but the other parents don't know that. The group decides to try vaping while there. You:**

   a. aren't comfortable with vaping, or with lying to your parents, but you don't want to lose your friends. You vape to fit in, and even pressure another friend who is also reluctant.

   b. don't feel comfortable, but pretend you are okay with the plan, then pretend you are sick that day so you don't have to go.

   c. tell your friends that you don't want to vape and will get in major trouble if your parents find out that you lied to them. You hope they won't end the friendship over your decision not to join them.

Quiz Results

If you answered mostly 'a,' then handling peer pressure may create a lot of stress and even some anxiety for you. The rest of this chapter will help you learn how to cope with peer pressure.

If you answered mostly 'b,' then you know what you want to do and what you don't, but you may not always know how to deal with friends putting pressure on you to do or say something that makes you uncomfortable. You will find tools for handling peer pressure in the pages ahead.

If you answered mostly 'c,' then you already have some good ideas about how to cope with peer pressure. But keep reading. You may learn even more tips!

Group Voice

While some groups of kids truly enjoy being in a group that's full of different voices and gives them the freedom to express themselves, many other groups expect everyone to follow some unwritten rules. These rules are part of the "group voice" defined earlier in the chapter, when the most vocal, popular, or powerful members of the group decide what is okay to think or do, and what isn't. Do you ever feel pressure to conform in order to keep your group of friends?

A positive or motivating group voice might give you the incentive you need to work harder or try something new and exciting.

When the group voice is negative and uncomfortable for you, it can become a problem. In some cases, you may feel like you are being forced to go along with the rules or risk losing your friends. Instead of going to a concert on a night before a major test, you may want to have a quiet night at home so you can study. Or maybe you want to spend time with your family on days when your group of friends choose to go out. How you handle these kinds of situations, and how the group responds, can make the difference between staying in the group or looking for new friends.

Sometimes a group of friends may push you to do things that could be dangerous, such as trying alcohol or hurting someone. Would you want to be part of that group so much that you go along with the pressure, even when you don't think the actions are right? If you find yourself in this position, it's time to think about a few things:

- Are there other kids in the group who don't want to participate, either? Would they support your decision to avoid doing these things?
- Why do you want to be part of this group or be friends with the members if they are putting pressure on you? If you go

William

William, age 14, liked his group of friends but dreaded Diego's yearly costume party. William knew that the party was safe and lots of his friends would be there, but he was always embarrassed to dress up. Plus, Diego and Timothy were the only ones who had a say in what the party's theme would be. Last year, everyone had to dress up as Disney characters. William knew that Diego and Timothy would decide the theme again this year, and the rest of the group would go along with it. No one wanted to risk speaking up and resisting the group voice, because everyone was worried that other kids would talk about them behind their back if they did.

This year, William was told to dress up as a famous person from history. William didn't want to offend his group of friends or have the guys talk negatively about him. He also didn't want to be kicked out of the group. This put intense peer pressure on William to go along with the plan. He decided to dress up, but he felt uncomfortable the whole night.

- ° If you were William, would you have dressed up and gone to the party even if you felt uncomfortable?
- ° If not, what would you have done instead? What would you have said to your group of friends?
- ° Is it okay to go along with the wishes of others sometimes, rather than risk offending them or being rejected?

along with the peer pressure in this group only because you aren't sure if you would be accepted in any other group, it may be time to speak with a parent, school counselor, or other trusted adult to get some guidance and support.

- Going along with harmful behaviors can change your future. You may be unnecessarily putting yourself at risk or even risking legal consequences.

Leaving a group of friends isn't easy. You may worry that you will be lonely without your social group, or that kids outside of your group will reject you because of negative things you might have done to be part of your current group. Don't let this stop you from making a courageous decision, though. Let others see who you really are when you're acting more naturally. Be kind and respectful, and be yourself. Hopefully, others will then be more accepting of you.

Group voice isn't always a negative thing. There may be cases when the group voice tells group members to work hard so that everyone gets into honors classes, for example. Maybe one or two members of a group decide to set aside time to practice soccer, a sport everyone in the group loves, so the group as a whole can improve in the game. A positive or motivating group voice might give you the incentive you need to work harder or try something new and exciting.

Saying 'No' to Negative Peer Pressure

It's not always easy to resist peer pressure, especially when you don't want to lose a friendship. If you're part of a group that prides itself on being cool and all group members make fun of other kids or break rules, it may be hard to stay friends if you don't conform. But it's important to remember that people who tease others or who take away your freedom to make choices for yourself aren't really friends. They are kids who only accept you if you act like them instead of being true to yourself. Keep this in mind when you're facing negative peer pressure. It may help you resist the pressure to conform.

Just because you avoid giving in to peer pressure from a group of friends, it doesn't mean you have to give up your friendships with everyone in the group. Sometimes there may be kids in the group who are really nice, even though they feel like they must follow the group's expectations. It is worth asking yourself if you can be friends with these kids outside of the group. Maybe you could form a new, more positive group together.

Some people only remain in a group because they fear being lonely otherwise. Lots of kids, teenagers, and adults are facing the same fear. You can still have friends and also resist peer pressure! Here are some tips for how to keep friends and stand up to peer pressure at the same time:

- If you belong to a group of friends who pressure you and are mean to others, respectfully and calmly let them know that you are not comfortable with these behaviors. You can then emphasize that you would like to stay friends if they stop their negative actions (if that's the case).

- Show respect to the others in your group, even if you're rejecting something they want you to do. It's fine for you to compromise and show flexibility sometimes. However, you may also need to let your group know that there are some things you won't do, such as hurtful or risky actions.

- Distract your group from the activities that make you uncomfortable. Try organizing a fun activity and inviting the whole group. Maybe some of the group members will come and learn to enjoy what you want to do!

- Try hanging out with some of the group members alone, so you have a close connection outside the group. Hopefully you can keep those friendships even if you end up leaving the larger group.

- Make friends with different people outside your group. Having a diverse group of friends is not only a great way to learn more about yourself and the world, but it also gives you friends to lean on if you decide you're not comfortable with a particular social group.

- Find kids who accept you for who you are. Maybe there are people you know from your sports team or from math club. Think about the people in your life who make you feel confident, accepted, and happy. Those are the kinds of people you want as friends.

If you belong to a group of friends who are fun, supportive, caring, and make you feel accepted, then dealing with occasional harmless peer pressure may not be as difficult. For example, if most of your friends want to go bowling on Sunday afternoon, but you would rather go to the mall, it's okay to be flexible. Some flexibility, and the ability to compromise, are essential in any friendship. In this situation, perhaps you can go bowling and then go to the mall on a different day.

On the other hand, if you always have to go along with the ideas and plans of others, and you don't feel like you have a say in what you do, this might not be the right group for you. Talk with a trusted adult about your feelings. This person may be able to help you to figure out if you should take a stand with your present group, start hanging out with just a few kids from the group, or branch out and make new friends.

> Just because you avoid giving in to peer pressure from a group of friends, it doesn't mean you have to give up your friendships with everyone in the group.

Why Am I Left Out?

Exclusion, or leaving someone out, sometimes happens accidentally, such as when you thought you had invited all of your friends

> *Friends may not always agree with each other, but they should basically like each other without pressuring the other person to change.*

to a party, but you overlooked one friend who you truly care about. Sometimes it happens because including everyone isn't practical. For example, if you only had permission to have three friends sleep over, you would have to choose who to invite. You could invite others another time. In these cases, no one is trying to intentionally hurt anyone's feelings.

There are times, though, when exclusion happens because a person doesn't want certain people to join in an activity. There are times when a group of kids don't want to let others into their group because they like the way the group is now and don't want to risk changing things by including others. Some kids, and even adults, exclude people because they don't understand them or their culture, or just view them as different. There are even times when exclusion occurs because of discrimination and negatively judging someone because of the group they belong to, their skin color, their religion, or other such attributes.

If you know that you have been excluding kids from joining your friendship circle, ask yourself why. Are you concerned that your friendship group will change? Are you worried that your friends will like the new kid more than they like you? Do you dislike change? Is the person someone you know is not respectful and kind? Once you know why you want to exclude someone, you can figure out if it's actually the right thing to do. If not, you can try to accept the new person and possibly develop a wonderful new friendship.

If your friends are trying to exclude someone from your group, it may be for similar reasons. You want your friends to know you respect their feelings, so listen to how they feel about the possibility of having another person hang out in your group. Can you come up with a way for your friends to feel comfortable with a new person? Can you talk with them about the positive effects of having good friends who are different? This may not always work. Some people may just not get along. But this doesn't mean you have to forget

Romey

Romey, age 11, had a close group of five friends. She loved hanging out with them. They laughed all the time and liked the same things. One day, Romey walked into her school cafeteria and invited her classmate, Liz, to come to her table. Liz was quiet and shy. Romey was curious about her. She always seemed to get good grades but never joined any school activities.

Romey and Liz talked all through lunch, and Romey was surprised to hear that Liz wanted to join a few school clubs to make friends. The problem was that after school Liz had to go home to help with her four younger siblings. Liz also shared that she was hoping to become an astronaut one day. Romey thought that was cool and enjoyed learning more about Liz.

When Romey's friends came to the table and saw Liz sitting there talking with Romey, they looked at each other and rolled their eyes. Romey got the message: her friends were annoyed. Romey introduced Liz, but her friends simply gave small smiles and sat at the other end of the long table. Despite their negative reaction, Romey continued her lunch with Liz. She felt that Liz was a nice person and would make a great friend.

- ° If you were Romey, how would you have handled the situation with your friends?
- ° Would you continue to get to know Liz, or return to hanging out just with your group?
- ° Would you avoid getting to know other kids for fear of getting into a conflict with your current friends?

Beckie

Beckie, age 12, recently started hanging out with Peter. They both enjoyed being friends and doing things such as rollerblading and playing video games together. A few months into their friendship, Beckie started to feel uncomfortable with some of the comments her friends, Miriam and Lettie, made. They told Beckie that it was weird to be friends with a boy and that they didn't want to hang around Peter, especially at the movies or while riding bikes. Miriam and Lettie gave Beckie a choice: They told her if she didn't stop spending so much time with Peter, they wouldn't hang out with her anymore.

Beckie was sad and upset. She didn't want to lose Peter, Miriam, or Lettie. She wasn't sure what to do. After talking with her parents and her school guidance counselor, Beckie decided to have a conversation with Miriam and Lettie. She stayed calm and used 'I' messages (see page 63) when she talked with them. After listening to their feelings, Beckie told Miriam and Lettie that she understood their comments and she wanted to stay friends with them. Beckie offered to hang out just with the two of them more often. Miriam and Lettie agreed that they wanted to keep their friendship with Beckie, too. They explained that they were worried that Beckie would spend so much time with Peter that she wouldn't have time for them anymore. That's where their peer pressure was coming from. After the conversation, all three girls felt much better, and Miriam and Lettie realized it was okay to have friends outside their group. They didn't pressure Beckie anymore to end her friendship with Peter, and Beckie made sure to spend time just with Miriam and Lettie again.

° If you were Beckie, Miriam, or Lettie, how would you have handled this situation?
° What would you have done if Miriam or Lettie insisted that you stop hanging out with Peter?

about being friends with someone new. You can still develop a friendship outside your group. Your true friends will, hopefully, accept your choice.

Positive Peer Pressure

As mentioned earlier in this chapter, sometimes peer pressure isn't negative. There are times when peer pressure can be a good thing. If your friends try to motivate you to take healthy risks and to have more confidence in yourself, it can feel uncomfortable or create anxiety. But it may be easier to try new activities once you realize that your friends believe in you and have your back. For example, if a friend keeps encouraging you to try out for a lead role in the school play, because she has seen how much acting and singing talent you have, perhaps this will give you the courage to try out and get a role! Even if you don't get a big role, or even get a part in the play at all, you may feel proud of yourself for stepping outside your comfort zone and trying something new.

Have you ever put positive peer pressure on a friend? Often people don't like to try new or unfamiliar things, or to stop doing things they're used to doing. They feel safe doing what they have always done. You may be able to help your friends feel comfortable stepping out of their own comfort zones. Life can be an adventure when you have good friends who encourage and support each other! Of course, be careful not to consistently pressure a friend, even if you're just trying to encourage that person. There can be a thin line between encouraging and nagging or insisting.

Are Friendships Worth It?

There are friendships that help you feel included, connected, and appreciated, and are tons of fun no matter your similarities or differences. In these friendships, you can hopefully be yourself and not feel pressure to change.

There are times, though, when you have to question whether friendships are really friendly at all. Here are some things to think about when deciding whether to stay in a friendship:

- Do you feel comfortable introducing your friend to others, such as your parents, or are you embarrassed about something? If you are embarrassed, is this something you need to work on, or is it something that may lead you to question the friendship?

- Do you share some common interests and enjoy time together doing those things?

- Even if you have different interests, is there acceptance, and enough that connects you that you feel like you can enjoy each other's company?

- Are you asked to reject other friends in order to keep the relationship?

- Are you asked to change or behave in a way that you don't like?

Friends may not always agree with each other, but they should basically like each other without pressuring the other person to change. Do you have friends who accept you and help you feel better when you're down? Are you that kind of friend to others?

Think about why you originally became friends with someone. Remember the good qualities and what brought you both together. Is your friend still the kind, fun, and respectful person you first met? Can you keep the closeness even if one or both of you start to change in some way? If you feel confined or you feel like the other person isn't supporting you, it may be time to take a friendship break. This means that you take some time away from your friend but keep open the possibility of re-connecting in the future. If you are both willing to accept each other's differences, perhaps you can work to continue the friendship, even if it has to change.

Call to Action

Think about whether you and your friends accept each other, despite your differences. Are there advantages to being a little different from one another? Do you know how to handle a situation where you feel forced to conform or do things that you aren't comfortable with in order to keep a friendship? How could you respectfully explain your discomfort to your friends while also letting them know that you want to be accepted for who you are, and that you don't want to do certain things? Take some time to write down a list of ideas for dealing with peer pressure situations like these. By doing this, you may be better prepared if you ever have to deal with something similar in the future.

7

FEELING ALONE

MOST PEOPLE LIKE TO KNOW THAT THEY HAVE FRIENDS, family, and others who care about them in their life. It's hard to go through life alone, and it can be fun to hang out with good friends. A close friend or a close group of friends can help you to feel included and supported when you need or want it. However, there may be times when you try to make friends, but certain kids just ignore you or walk away, leaving you feeling lonely, rejected, sad, or angry. You may decide that you don't want to be friends with kids who act in that way, but it can still hurt.

Loneliness can happen when you feel misunderstood and disconnected. You might even feel lonely when you're surrounded by friends. If you have to pretend to like certain activities, or if you aren't acting like your true self, you may feel lonely even when others are with you. Have you ever felt this way?

In this chapter you will learn ways to handle feelings of loneliness and rejection. You will also read about why being alone, at times, may not be such a bad thing. Before moving ahead, though, take a few minutes to answer the questions on the next page. As you think about your answers, ask yourself how you feel about being alone as well as how you cope with feelings of loneliness and rejection.

Quiz

1. **You want to become friends with Margaret, but she likes sports and you like art. Margaret likes to hang out in groups and you like to spend time together one-on-one. When you ask Margaret to hang out with you and work on an art project, she politely says no. You:**

   a. decide that Margaret is rejecting you, which makes you feel lonely, sad, and even mad.

   b. realize that you don't have a lot in common with Margaret, so you stop talking to her, but then feel lonely.

   c. look for other friends who like the same things as you, but still sometimes try to get together with Margaret.

2. **When you realize that you were left out of a party or a get-together, you:**

   a. assume that the other kids don't like you, which makes you feel so sad and lonely that you start crying.

   b. still hang out with the other kids, because they seem nice and usually do include you, but you are hurt.

   c. stay calm and watch to see if this is a pattern or isolated event before deciding how to react.

3. **Your friend tells you that he feels like you would rather be alone than hang out with him. You:**

   a. tell your friend that he's wrong and that he's just making stuff up.

   b. think about what your friend is saying, but you believe he's wrong, so you don't try to change your behavior.

c. listen carefully to why your friend feels that way and explain why you have been spending more time alone lately.

4. **Your best friend seems to have a new best friend. You try to join both of them at recess, but you get the feeling that they don't want you there with them. You:**

a. get angry and tell other kids how annoying your former best friend is.

b. are confused and feel lonely. You sit alone outside, hoping that your former best friend comes over to spend time with you.

c. realize that you can't restrict who your friend spends time with. You invite your friend over to your house to see if you can reconnect one-on-one. Then you try to find an activity that your best friend, his new friend, and you can all enjoy together.

5. **You think that everyone at school seems to have good friends, except you. This makes you feel invisible. No one tries to include you in games at recess and you are the last person chosen for a group activity in class. You:**

a. feel rejected, lonely, and sad. You rush home after school every day and give up on making friends.

b. talk with a grown-up and think about ways to get to know other kids, but you are too nervous to give them a try.

c. listen to the advice of trusted adults and try some new friendship strategies. You start conversations with classmates on topics that interest you both.

Quiz Results

If you answered mostly 'a,' then you may be feeling lonely and confused about how to fit in with other kids. In this chapter, you can find some useful tips to help you to cope with loneliness, and even help you enjoy being alone sometimes. You will also find ways to help yourself to establish connections with others.

If you answered mostly 'b,' then you are aware of how you feel and are in the process of figuring out how to connect with others so you are accepted and included.

If you answered mostly 'c,' then you may already know how to find good friends and cope with situations where you feel rejected or left out. As you continue reading, you will find lots of tips to help you deal with your feelings.

Staying Strong

If you have ever been excluded from a group or had a friend who seemed to reject you, you are not alone. This happens to lots of kids, and it can lead to hurt feelings and even self-doubts. Some kids wonder if there is something wrong with them, since others don't seem to want to hang out with them.

Loneliness can happen when you feel misunderstood and disconnected. You might even feel lonely when you're surrounded by friends.

In the next section of this chapter, you will have the opportunity to think about possible reasons you feel left out or rejected. But before getting started, it's important for you to find ways to feel good about yourself no matter how many friends you have.

Even if you're alone, you don't necessarily need to feel lonely. Being alone can be fun sometimes. If you are alone, do you:

- enjoy having time to yourself, even though you also want friends?
- find that you like having the time to focus on your imagination and your hobbies?
- enjoy trying new experiences, even on your own?
- appreciate yourself and consider yourself a good person?

If you have high self-esteem, meaning that you feel good about yourself, then sometimes it may be great to have time to yourself. Think about the fun things you can you do when you are alone. Having some ideas will help you enjoy the moments you have to yourself.

Solomon

Solomon, age 11, really liked having close friends. He liked hanging out in groups or one-on-one. One day at school he suddenly noticed that kids were excluding him from activities. This made him feel angry and insecure, and he wondered if there was something wrong with him. Solomon spent all his free time trying to get his friends back. He even bought them snacks and other things they wanted, but nothing was working.

Solomon soon realized why his friends were ignoring him. They had recently asked him to pretend to like a particular girl and then dump her, and Solomon had refused. Also, his friends had asked him to give them the questions and answers for a science test that he would be taking before them. Again, Solomon refused their request. After these two events, his friends had started to distance themselves from him.

Solomon felt embarrassed being alone at school, and he felt sad when he saw other kids laughing and having fun without him. At first, he thought about refusing to go to school. But then he spoke to his parents about the situation and realized that true friends wouldn't have asked him to do something mean to another person and they wouldn't reject him for deciding not to share test information. Solomon decided to find new friends, but also to stay open to working out friendships with his old friends if they made an effort to do so. During his alone time, he decided he would try to do some pottery, something he had always enjoyed but had little time for in the past.

° How would you feel about being excluded?
° If you were Solomon, what would you have done in the same situation?

If you are ignored by your friends, and you don't feel that it's because you acted in a disrespectful or hurtful way, you can still feel proud of your behavior, even if you're feeling disappointed that you were excluded. Remember that you don't ever have to do things that you know aren't right or that make you feel unsafe or very uncomfortable just to keep a friendship. While you are using some of the tips that you read about earlier in this book to make friends, try to be your own best friend, too.

Here are some ways to feel good about yourself, even when you are alone:

- Remind yourself that you have many good qualities and can be a good friend to people who appreciate you.

- Spend time with those people who do appreciate you.

- Make a list of your strengths, for example "I'm kind, thoughtful, funny, and I like playing soccer." Look at this list when you're feeling down.

- Be kind to yourself by doing some things that you enjoy.

- Use your quiet time to do something that you may never have had time to do before, but always wanted to try.

Getting through a lonely time can be difficult, but it can help you become a stronger, more confident person when you realize that you are a good person who doesn't give in to negative peer pressure in order to have friends. Try to develop friendships where you don't have to change who you are to fit in.

Why Exclusion Happens

Exclusion can happen for many reasons, not all of which are meant to be hurtful. Sometimes, as you read in the last chapter, a person may be excluded from an activity because there is a limit

Darlene

Darlene, age 12, was often teased in school. Kids made fun of her for her acne. She was working hard to clear up her skin and was regularly seeing a dermatologist for help. Some kids also made fun of her accent and they often told her that no one liked her.

Darlene didn't do anything to bring on this negative attention, and she often cried when she was teased. When Kristen invited her to a party, Darlene thought she might be able to make some friends. She was so happy!

But at the party, kids bossed her around, telling her to get them snacks and drinks. They also made fun of her new dress, which she was proud of and had made herself. Finally, Darlene decided to leave. She told the other kids that she didn't need to be treated that way and said that she could have been a great friend to them.

Darlene texted her mom and was picked up. She and her parents planned to speak with the principal about how kids in school had been treating Darlene. Darlene was also going to try to convince her parents to move so she could start at a new school and meet different kids. But the next day, Darlene was approached by two kids from the party. They both apologized for how they had treated her. They said they thought about what she said at the party and respected her for speaking up without insulting anyone. During the next few months, Darlene became close friends with these two girls.

° What would you have done if you were constantly being teased or mistreated like Darlene?
° What do you think of what Darlene said at the party?

to how many people can join in. In this type of situation, it may be a good idea to invite different friends at different times so everyone feels included. Expecting that you will always be the kid picked for all activities, could put too much pressure on your friend to exclude others. There may also be situations where kids are accidentally excluded. If a friend invites everyone to come over to his house to hang out after school and one friend didn't get the message, she may think she is being purposely excluded and feel hurt and rejected.

Exclusion can happen for many reasons, not all of which are meant to be hurtful.

Unlike Darlene, some kids give the impression that they want to be excluded, even though they don't. Why would someone do this? Possibly to try to hide their true feelings of insecurity, hurt, or perceived rejection. For example, you hear your close friend telling a bunch of kids in class that she and her family are moving at the end of the year. You are sad to learn that she's moving, but you are also very hurt that she didn't tell you first. After all, you have been good friends for many years. Out of hurt, you approach your friend and say, "Whatever! Have fun!" and walk away. Your friend is left wondering why you would say that, especially if she didn't mean to keep the news about her move from you. Maybe she thought you were part of the group she was talking to when she shared that news, or she was very uncomfortable telling you she was moving because she would miss you so much, and she thought a general announcement would be easier for her. By pulling away from your friend, she may end up feeling that she's being rejected. She may also think that you no longer want to be part of her life. In reality, you do want to be friends but don't know how to process your hurt feelings. This miscommunication and the resulting hurt feelings could end the friendship. Trying some friendship strategies could help work things out, if you want to stay connected. Here are some tips:

- Think about your true feelings. Are you really angry? Or are you hurt or scared?

- Think about how you might clear up any misunderstanding. Would you be willing to speak honestly with your friend?

- If you really do want to stay friends and be included, then calm down, avoid insults or accusations, and try to respectfully talk things out. It can be helpful to put off having a conversation while you are really upset. Try talking with a trusted adult first to get some advice on how to handle the situation in a calm and respectful way.

If you are trying to fit in but believe that you are purposely being excluded by your friends, think about these questions:

- How willing are you to be flexible and compromise with your friends when deciding what to do together? Have you been insisting on doing everything your way, and do you think that could be a reason you've been excluded? Should you have a conversation with your friends to figure it out?

- Is your effort to fit in only making you feel uncomfortable and lonely? Are you fearful of rejection if you act like yourself? Is it time to find new friends who are caring and accepting of you?

- If you are excluded from certain activities that have a limited number of participants, but you are included in other activities, are you okay with staying in the group? Do you also want to look for other friends so that you are more likely to have someone to hang out with when you are available?

No matter why exclusion happens, it's important to try to understand the reasons behind it and take steps to change your situation for the better. Sometimes this means working things out with your friend, sometimes it means staying close but changing the relationship, and, at times, it means taking a break from the friendship.

When to Take a Break

How do you know when it's time to take a break from a friendship? If you realize that you are having to completely change who you are in order to stay friends, or you don't feel good when you are with kids in your group, it may be time to step away, especially if you've tried to talk with your friends and be accepted for who you are. If you make the choice to take a break, what can you do to move forward? Are there other friends who you can spend more time with now? Are there new activities you want to try? Would you like to spend more time with your family? You may also want to keep in mind that your friendship could get closer again in the future, because people can change!

Try to develop friendships where you don't have to change who you are to fit in.

When you're trying to move forward after ending a friendship, thinking over these questions can help:

- You may feel down over the end of your friendship, but do you feel calmer without the pressure of trying to make the friendship work? Do you feel free to be who you are?

- Think about other people you know. (This would be a good time to go back to the circles of people in your life.) Who can you reach out to in order to start a new friendship?

- What did you learn from your past friendship? If you know what went wrong, how can you try to avoid a similar situation with a new friend?

- What hobbies could fill your time?

- Are there clubs at school or at the local community center that you can join to meet new people?

If you are looking for friends but can't seem to find the right friends for you, it's a good idea to speak with a trusted adult, such as a parent, school guidance counselor, school psychologist, or teacher. They have likely been around lots of kids and may have great tips on how you can try to make friends with people who will accept you and who you will accept in return.

Call to Action

How do you decide whether you should try to keep a particular friendship, or if it's time to move on? Try listing the pros and cons of keeping the friendship, then think about how you feel being in the friendship, and how you would feel if you stepped away. Are you lonely even when you're with your friend because you don't feel appreciated or understood? Are you excluded sometimes? Would you miss your friend, and are there other, more comfortable ways you could spend time together? Think about these questions and your pros and cons before you decide to take a friendship break. If you are confused about what to do, try talking over your feelings with a trusted adult.

8

FRIENDSHIPS AND SOCIAL MEDIA

COMMUNICATING ON SOCIAL MEDIA OR THROUGH video games can lead to close connections among friends who have common interests. While not everyone has access to social media, or permission to use it, many kids do, and spend lots of time on it. Unfortunately, as you probably already know, social media can sometimes be harmful. In the worst situations, kids are bullied or connect with people who pretend to be someone else and have bad intentions. Learning about the benefits and the risks of using social media can help to keep you safe. For the purposes of this chapter, the term 'social media' will refer to ways that you can socialize with others through technology.

In this chapter, you will read about some of the positive parts of social media—getting to know others better, keeping in touch when you're apart from friends, etc. But you will also have the opportunity to think about some of the drawbacks. There can be risks to over-sharing, miscommunication, and spending too much time communicating through a screen at times when you could have been hanging out with others in person. This chapter will help you to think about how you socialize with others through social media. Has it been helpful and positive, or have you been hurt or accidentally hurt others? This chapter won't tell you whether to use social media, but it will give you some things to think about when you look at your phone, laptop, or other device.

Before reading further, take a few minutes to answer the questions on the next page. This quiz will give you a chance to think about how social media may impact your friendships and to reflect on ways social media can be helpful or hurtful.

Quiz

1. **While in a group text, you are surprised to read that a few friends are ranking classmates on a variety of different factors. Lots of people are able to read this, so you:**

   a. decide you can be more popular by answering all of the questions, such as who is the ugliest and the smartest. After all, not all of the categories are negative!

   b. read the texts with interest and curiosity but feel a little uncomfortable about answering because you know that judging and ranking others can be hurtful.

   c. text the others and admit that the ranking seems fun, but say that it's better to stick to positive things so no one gets hurt.

2. **A kid from class you like sends you silly pictures, which you enjoy. However, one day, he asks you to send him a picture of you that makes you uncomfortable. You:**

   a. agree to do this, because you can't risk disappointing him and losing the friendship.

   b. joke and say something like, "Ha ha, that's funny," and pretend that you think he was just joking.

   c. decide to wait until the next day, and then tell him that you liked the silly pictures he sent, but you won't be sending the picture he asked for because it makes you feel uncomfortable. You hope he understands and respects your decision and feelings. If not, you are okay losing the friendship.

3. You are playing a video game with a few friends, and each person is playing from their own home. When another kid joins, you assume that she's a friend of another friend, so you accept her. One day, she suggests that you e-mail each other, and you agree. Then she starts asking you very personal questions, such as your address. You:

   a. assume that she must be nice since she joined the video game, so you give her the information.

   b. ignore the request, hoping she doesn't ask again.

   c. speak with your parents because you are very uncomfortable. You decide to also check with your friends to see if anyone really knows this person outside of the gaming group. You know that safety has to come before making or keeping a new friend.

4. You and your friends text every afternoon. It's a ton of fun, and all of you make plans for getting together on the weekends. However, you are so busy chatting that you aren't getting all of your homework done. You:

   a. ignore the homework. You try to only focus on the fun you are having.

   b. don't know how to get offline sooner to give yourself homework time. You feel stressed and aren't sure what to do about it.

   c. tell your friends that you don't want to sign off, but you have to get your homework done. You hope that either they feel the same way, or they will respect your decision and not leave you out of future plans.

5. You text a friend to let her know that you felt that her class presentation was hilarious. You thought she would like that, but the next day, your friend seems to purposely ignore you and later tells you that you were mean to trash the presentation. You:

a. are confused but also hurt that she was acting so cold. You just roll your eyes and decide she's weird.

b. feel bad that your friend misunderstood your intended compliment, but don't know how to deal with the situation now.

c. find time to talk with her and work hard to clarify that you meant your comment as a compliment. Then you listen to her talk about how she felt and apologize if it's appropriate.

Quiz Results

If you answered mostly 'a,' then handling social media and connections with friends online may create confusion and even anxiety for you. As you read through this chapter, you can learn more about how to cope with this topic.

If you answered mostly 'b,' then you understand what you want to do and what you don't want to do online, but you may not always know how to actually handle stressful situations on social media. Keep reading to learn some important tools for handling social media in friendships.

If you answered mostly 'c,' then you already have a lot of information about how to use social media and how to avoid or deal with any difficulties. As you continue reading, you may learn even more!

Positive Uses of Social Media

Social media, texting, and phone calls can help you to connect with friends and even family members. For example, with a smartphone, you could contact a friend or relative who moved to another country. No airfare or travel time is required!

Smartphone and computer technology have also helped to speed up communication. In the past, it would take time to write and mail letters and wait for a reply. It was faster to make a phone call, but long-distance calls were expensive, and you couldn't talk face-to-face. Today, it's much easier to connect and remain close with family and friends. Even if you live far away, you can send and receive messages in a matter of seconds and see each other as you talk by using your device.

During times when you have to stay home for a long period of time, such as during a pandemic, you may not be able to see your friends in person. Talking, video chatting, or texting with others can help you to feel connected and less isolated and lonely. This could be true for shorter periods of separation too, such as if you are home sick or if there's a snowstorm. However, even at these times, the pros and cons of using social media need to be considered.

Having the ability to connect with people immediately can allow you to stay up to date on the latest gossip, share news, or even to ask questions and hopefully get answers about school projects or assignments. It can also decrease feelings of isolation if you are homesick while away from your family or you can't travel to see loved ones. Having the ability to chat with multiple people at once also makes it easier to make plans for getting together in person.

Another benefit of using technology to communicate is that it gives you the opportunity to think before you "speak." You

> Having the ability to connect with people immediately can decrease feelings of isolation if you are homesick or you can't travel to see loved ones.

Gloria

Gloria, age 11, enjoyed spending summers visiting with her old friend, Mae, who moved with her family to another state three years ago. Gloria had remained close with Mae by texting and doing video chats. With the help of the latest technology, Gloria even got a tour of Mae's newly decorated room.

During the summer, Gloria went to visit Mae for a month. Gloria had lots of fun but missed her parents. She called her mom and they decided to have face-to-face calls every few days. This helped Gloria feel like her parents and her little brother weren't so far away. Many years later, when Gloria left for college, she continued using technology to stay connected with her family and friends. For Gloria, technology also allowed her to bond with friends by playing multi-player games, texting, and video chatting. If Gloria's family or friends wanted to share news with her, or she had something to show someone, such as her latest artwork, she was able to do so quickly and easily, no matter the distance between herself and the other people.

° If you were separated from people who you care about, could you use social media to remain connected?
° Could social media decrease feelings of being lonely or homesick?

can read a comment, pause, and spend time thinking about how you want to respond before texting back. When face-to-face, people usually want immediate responses to comments. Even during traditional phone conversations, when one person stops talking, another person begins. There isn't much time to pause and think. If you are uncertain about how to respond to someone's comments over text, you could even ask your parents or other trusted adult for ideas on how best to respond.

Since social media allows you to communicate quickly with a large group of people, another of its advantages is that you can share your goals and see if others share them as well. Perhaps you want to work on climate change, raise money for a charity, or participate in a walk-a-thon. You don't have to contact people one at a time. It's often easy to reach lots of people at once to see if they want to join you as you work to make the world a better place!

Sometimes you can save time by communicating via social media rather than trying to plan the best time to talk with someone. Imagine if you just want your mom to know that you got an 'A' on your essay in English class, but she's in a meeting when you're free to contact her. You might decide to send a quick text to your mom to share the good news, and she can read it when she's available. A quick text back from your mother later can let you know her reaction. When you have time and are home, you can talk more about it.

Drawbacks of Social Media

Understanding the drawbacks to social media can help you be more aware of possible problems and dangers. What are the drawbacks that you need to know about? Here are some general areas of caution.

Miscommunication is one common issue kids face on social media, particularity when texting. There may be times when someone is trying to be funny, for example, but it comes off as insulting to the reader. When you can't see the person or people you are speaking with, or hear their tone of voice, it's easy to take things the wrong way.

Here are a few other reasons miscommunication may happen more often online than face-to-face:

- The writer may not give you as many details as he would in person since typing takes longer than talking, so you may not get all of the information you need.

- Without hearing someone's tone of voice, it's not always easy to know if the person is joking or serious.

- Sometimes texts can be cryptic on purpose, if the sender is trying to make sure other readers, like parents, won't understand the message.

- Without knowing where someone is when texting, or what happened just beforehand, some statements can seem confusing. For example, if your friend suddenly typed "I'm so hot!" when you were just texting about a homework assignment, the comment would make a lot more sense if you knew that he was out for a walk with his dog on a particularly hot evening.

Another kind of miscommunication involves sending information to the wrong person. There are times when someone might want to text one person, but accidentally sends a message to someone else. This can be no big deal, or a major issue, depending on what the message was and who it was sent to. Be extra careful when messaging: reread your messages, check for autocorrect, which can change the meaning of your words, double check who the message is going to, and then send your message if you think it's ready to be seen.

Focus on building people up rather than knocking them down, whether you are communicating online or in person.

Joshua

Joshua, age 12, loved to joke around. He knew everyone in his sixth-grade class and often got together with his friends. At home, Joshua was often texting friends or on group chats. One day, he shared with everyone on a group chat that he thought Caroline was a "walking brain."

A number of kids immediately liked that comment. Then George added that Caroline has always been way too serious, and she should "lighten up." Other kids quickly shared their thoughts as well. Some of the comments became very negative. For example, Vanessa said that Caroline was one of the least liked kids in sixth grade.

Joshua was surprised by Vanessa's comment, but decided to ignore it. He wasn't sure what to do. Caroline's best friend, Shiana, was on the group chat and shared the information from that chat with Caroline because she wanted her friend to know what others were saying about her. The next day in school, Caroline was absent. When she returned later in the week, she didn't look at anyone. Joshua asked Shiana if Caroline was upset about anything. Shiana told him that Caroline heard about the texting and was hurt by the remarks about her. Joshua went over to Caroline and said that he didn't agree with Vanessa's comment and he thought of her as a friend. Caroline told Joshua that Vanessa's comment was really hurtful, but his words also hurt her a lot. Joshua was surprised. He reviewed what he wrote. He meant that she was a "walking brain" in a good way. She studied a lot and got good grades. Joshua really admired Caroline's dedication to her schoolwork. He just wanted her to have more fun because he felt bad that she spent so much time studying.

- ° Can you see why Caroline was hurt?
- ° What can Joshua do to fix the situation?
- ° What can you do to prevent such a situation from occurring?

Oversharing private information is another very important reason to be cautious online. Some kids feel comfortable texting private information (or even personal pictures) to someone or multiple people who they think they can trust. This is something to avoid, because you can't take back the information or pictures once you send them to others. Always remember that even though you may be alone when you send out something personal, you are connected to those on the other side of the site or chat. There is always a possibility that your information may be shared with others or used in ways that you did not intend.

In addition to oversharing and miscommunication, think about whether you are excluding others on social media. For example, if you invite lots of people into a group chat, but then share information about a party that you are having and list only a few of the kids who you want to come, those not included may feel left out. It's kind of like putting up a big billboard by the side of a major highway announcing your party, but then listing who is not invited. Feelings can easily be hurt, and you may not even know it. And the people reading the information may never tell you that your words hurt them. In order to avoid hurting someone, think about the ways others might interpret your words and the possible unintended consequences.

Another issue that can come up on social media is bullying. Bullying, of course, doesn't only happen online. It can happen at school or at the playground, or anywhere else you encounter others. But bullying on social media might happen at times when it wouldn't happen in person. Some people find it easier to say mean and disrespectful things from behind a computer or smartphone instead of directly to someone's face. Using insulting words or sending pictures or videos that make fun of another person can lead to real pain and even affect the self-esteem of the target. If you end up humiliating, embarrassing, or upsetting someone online, it could lead to a person feeling overwhelmed. If the person ends up feeling depressed and alone, this can lead to serious consequences.

If you ever have the urge to tease or even bully, or see bullying happen, put yourself in the target's shoes. How would you feel? Even if you might have thought the teasing was funny, consider the possibility that the other person might feel rejected and upset instead. Also, people could see your behavior as bullying, and your reputation, not just the reputation of the person you're talking about, could be harmed.

Some kids find it easier to pick on someone over social media because they don't have to see the pain in the person's eyes. Remember, though, that pain is still pain, whether you see it happening or not. Be proud of yourself. Be an upstander. Focus on building people up rather than knocking them down, whether you are communicating online or in person.

There is another important topic to cover in this section. What if you're online and meet someone you don't know? The person might tell you that he is in your grade and has similar interests. How do you know if he is telling the truth? In a case like this, make sure your parents or the other trusted adults in your life know who you are communicating with online. Why? Sometimes, while online, some grown-ups may pretend to be kids so they can take advantage of children. They may want an unhealthy connection with you, or they may want to learn personal information about your family. This type of behavior is very serious and never appropriate. It's important, as you probably already know, that you should never give a stranger online your real name or any information about you, such as your birthday or address. And of course, never do anything a stranger says: in fact, you should stop speaking with the person right away and tell a trusted adult immediately. While on social media, always be aware of who you're speaking with and what you're sharing.

Time to Disconnect?

Spend some time thinking about whether you should be online as much as you are. Do you feel pressure to constantly check your

While not everyone has access to social media, or permission to use it, many kids do, and spend lots of time on it. Learning about the benefits and the risks of using social media can help to keep you safe.

social media or texts because you are afraid of missing something important from a friend? Do you feel that you're always so busy documenting events (taking pictures or videos to later share) that you aren't really focusing on being in the moment? Then you may want to consider disconnecting for a while. Perhaps you can try getting together with friends when possible, or doing something outside, reading a great book, practicing music, or doing an art project.

Social media can be complicated. When you are online, remember the information presented here. Enjoy connecting with your friends and family, but also be aware of how words and actions online affect others. And always remember to stay safe and speak up when you see concerning behavior. Take a break, sometimes, to reconnect with yourself and to spend time with your friends and family in person when you can.

Call to Action

How much pressure do you feel to keep checking social media? What would your life be like if you disconnected for a week or two, or just more often each week? Decide how long you would like to take a break from using your social media, then give it a try. Let your friends and family know first, so they don't think that you are purposely ignoring them. After your break, think about how you feel. Are you calmer and less stressed, or do you miss it? Maybe both? When you do get back on social media, you may be able to find a better balance.

9

CHANGE OVER TIME

AS YOU GET OLDER, YOUR INTERESTS, SENSE OF HUMOR, and even personality may change. You might go from being shy to outgoing, or the opposite. You may decide you prefer to hang out in large groups or with just a few close friends. As you change, friendships may change, too.

Do you have any friends that you made years ago? If so, has the friendship changed at all? Imagine having a close friend you made when you were five years old. Now, imagine having that same friend when you are 10 or 15. Over the years, you have both probably changed and may change even more. Depending on how your interests and preferences evolve, you and your friend could stay close or grow apart.

In this chapter, you will read about some ways to keep close friendships, even when you and your friends are going through changes. Your friendships may end up being different than before, but they can still be meaningful and fun.

Before you move forward, take a few minutes to answer the questions on the next page. This quiz is designed to help you think about how to keep your longtime friends and grow together. Knowing how changing interests and personalities can affect friendships may help you cope if this happens.

Quiz

1. **One of your old friends starts hanging out with other kids. He still gets together with you, but you're upset that you don't spend as much time together anymore. You:**

   a. tell him that he's not being a good friend because he's excluding you.

   b. don't know how to handle the situation, so you keep your feelings of hurt and jealousy private.

   c. find a time to talk with your friend about how you feel. You tell him that you value the friendship but understand that both of you will want to hang out with other people sometimes. This way, you can make new friends, too.

2. **Your friend since kindergarten tells you she thinks you're both too old now to be playing board games. She says that video games and social media are cooler. Your feelings are hurt, and you disagree with her. You:**

   a. cry because you feel rejected. You stop socializing with other friends because you are afraid they will also reject you because of your interests.

   b. try to get into video games and social media so you can stay friends. You decide never to discuss board games again.

   c. still hang out with your old friend, and you both find ways to compromise: sometimes you play board games together, and other times, you do what your friend prefers.

3. **You feel that you no longer have much in common with an old friend. He's nice, but you want to hang out with new friends that share similar interests. You:**

   a. ignore your old friend, in hopes that he finds new friends.

   b. don't want to hurt his feelings, so you tell him that you are too busy to see him, but that you do want to get together at some point.

   c. have an honest conversation with your friend about still staying close but also branching out and meeting new people.

4. **You and your best friend have been close since you were toddlers. Now that you are both 11, you spend a lot of time talking about the future. You talk about going to the same college, maybe being roommates, traveling to different countries together, and even living next door to one another. During a recent conversation, your friend surprisingly said, "Stop! This is too much. You're a great friend, but we don't have to do everything together." You:**

   a. are hurt and angry. You immediately say, "I just said those things because I know you don't have a lot of friends, and I was just being nice."

   b. feel embarrassed and say, "Just joking! I sometimes want my own space, too."

   c. let your friend know you understand that she felt you were going too far planning your lives together. You clarify that you were joking, and while you hope you will have lots of experiences together in the future, you also want to do some new things on your own.

5. You and your longtime friend used to like drawing, baking, and making fun videos where both of you would sing and dance. Now, however, you spend more time playing soccer and hanging out with your teammates, while your friend isn't a soccer player and prefers to sew and hang out with friends from the theater club. You don't see each other very much anymore You:

a. decide you are too different to stay friends. When she asks to hang out, you keep telling her that you are busy, so you don't outright reject her.

b. still see each other once in a while, but you spend your time together trying to convince her to try out for the soccer team.

c. know that your friend doesn't like soccer, but you still think she's nice. You sometimes get together and do activities that you both enjoy.

Quiz Results

If you answered mostly 'a,' then trying to maintain a friendship over the years as you grow and change may make you uncomfortable and can be confusing. You will get an opportunity to learn how to cope with changes in your friendships as you read this chapter.

If you answered mostly 'b,' then you understand your feelings about your changing friendships and are trying to figure out how to handle them. Read on for some important tools you can use to handle long-term friendships.

If you answered mostly 'c,' then you may already have a good understanding about how to cope with changes among your friends! As you continue reading, you will probably learn even more.

Staying Connected

Since there's a good chance that you and your friend will change as you get older, you may need to be patient and flexible as you figure out how to maintain your connection. You might start to enjoy new hobbies or interests, but your friend may not change, or may prefer different activities from what you now like to do.

In the following section, you will read about how to handle changing interests between you and your friends. But first, take some time to think about all the reasons people become friends. For instance, did you become friends with someone because that person was kind, funny, and smart? Does that friend still have those characteristics? If the answer is yes, consider these questions:

- How can you still enjoy each other's company even though some of your interests and even social preferences may have changed?

- Does your friendship mean enough to you that you want to work to keep it, even if it's different now?

- How can you build on what originally brought the two of you together? For example, if you first met doing volunteer work, perhaps you and your friend can get involved in another charity that you are both enthusiastic about.

Longtime friends, and even new friends, may sometimes need to work on their friendship, but it's often worth the effort to stay connected if:

- you like the other person, despite the fact that your interests are changing or somewhat different.

- your friend appreciates you and you appreciate your friend.

- your friend has been with you so long that she know lots of things about you and almost seems like a part of your family.

Scott

When Scott and Michael were five, they lived in the same neighborhood and used to play catch in Scott's backyard. They also loved to play hide-and-seek. However, by the time they were 10, things changed. Michael spent a lot of time focused on robotics, and Scott was involved in student government. Soon, they didn't see each other as much and started drifting apart.

Scott missed Michael's friendship. He spoke with his dad about it. Scott's father helped him to focus on what he still liked about Michael. Scott remembered he and Michael had similar personalities and got along well. A few days later, Scott decided to invite Michael over to his home. They talked about what they both enjoyed and decided they could do those things together. Scott learned that he and Michael still had some common interests and shared a similar sense of humor. They realized that they still could hang out and have fun. In fact, they began to talk even more than they used to because they were also sharing new ideas and experiences with each other.

- ° If you were Scott, would you have slowly moved away from Michael and made new friends?
- ° Could you see the benefit of keeping old friends, while also moving toward making new ones?

As you decide whether or not to work on and continue an evolving friendship, think about the reasons you would or wouldn't want to keep that person in your life. If you still like, respect, and care about each other, even if you don't have as much in common, it may be worth sticking together. And as you grow into adulthood, you'll have a friend to share your memories!

Since there's a good chance that you and your friend will change as you get older, you may need to be patient and flexible as you figure out how to maintain your connection.

It may not always be possible to stay close with an old friend, and there are times when a friend becomes a close acquaintance. If this happens to you, it's possible you will reconnect in a different way over time. If you need to, take time to grow and let your old friend grow, too. Maybe you need some distance for now, but think about whether you can still enjoy spending time together occasionally, to keep up your connection.

Changing Interests

As previously discussed, longtime friends sometimes develop different interests. It can be hard to stay close if they no longer have things in common and are busy with their separate lives. In cases like this, keeping up an old friendship can take work. It can be easy to drift apart. You may suddenly realize that you were so busy that you went months without seeing or hanging out with your old friend. However, making sure that you get together regularly can make the difference between losing or keeping your friendship.

Some kids want all of their friends to be very similar and they end long-time friendships if differences come up. They may want all their friends to be athletes, or funny, or involved in the same activities, but it can be interesting and fun to have a variety of different friends, whether it's an old friend who changed or a new person. When you're making new friends, you may meet people who lived

> *There are times when a friend becomes a close acquaintance. Later, you may find a way to reconnect.*

in another country or have a different cultural background. Others may have moved from another state. There is so much diversity in the world, and it can be very rewarding to make friends with people from all walks of life. It can also be rewarding to stay close to old friends who aren't exactly the same as you but are trustworthy, respectful, and interesting.

If your old friend and you now have different interests, you may wonder why it's worth keeping the friendship. Why not just move on and establish new friendships with kids who are more similar to you? Only you can answer this question. Look back to the earlier part of this chapter to spend some time thinking about why it may be good to hold on to an old friend.

If you and your friend have developed different interests but you do want to stay close, here are suggestions that could help:

- Be open to learning about your friend's new interests.
- Be open to sharing your new interests.
- Be open to learning about how your friend's thinking has changed.
- Share your changing thoughts and beliefs with your friend.
- Let your friend know what you are doing these days and why you enjoy it.
- If you are open to trying a new activity or going to an event with your friend, ask if you can join. This can be a great way to experience new things together.
- Invite your friend to come to your game or other event.

Can you think of other ways to be creative in maintaining your old friendships? Sometimes it's well worth the effort to stay close.

Taking a Friendship Break

You have had the chance to read about lots of reasons to keep friendships, even as you or your friend change. However, sometimes staying close with a friend is hard to do, lots of work, and may not feel right to you. At times, you may need a friendship break. For instance, if you or your friend expect to always socialize one-on-one, this possessiveness can hurt the friendship. It can stop both of you from growing and having other friendships. It may even lead to one of you ending the friendship because you feel unable to make new connections with others or try new activities. Rather than just ending the friendship, first try talking it out; maybe you can maintain the friendship but give each other space to be more independent and connect with others as well.

There are other reasons why friendships might end. Perhaps you (or your friend) want to join a group of kids, and your longtime friendship no longer fits the image of who you are and who you want to hang out with, so you decide to stop being friends. If you are the one ending the friendship, here are some things to think about before you move ahead:

- Do you really want to end the friendship, or do you feel pressured to do so by your new friends? If you feel pressured, think about how you can be true to yourself and do what you feel is right.

- Is your new group of friends the right friendship group for you? Will you lose these new friends if you stay close with your old one?

- Does your old friend accept that you need time to develop new friendships? If so, it may be easier to maintain your old friendship! Hopefully, your new friends will see that you can give them lots of time even though you also are keeping close to your old friend.

Carly

Carly, age 11, had been friends with Maya since second grade. Suddenly, though, Carly was feeling held back by Maya. The popular kids in the grade were now hanging out more with Carly and she was finally feeling accepted by them. However, Maya kept criticizing her for being friends with them. Carly felt that Maya was just jealous.

Maya repeatedly warned Carly that the influence of the new group was changing Carly, and not in a good way. Maya told Carly to think about the choices she was making. Maya knew that Carly had always been a fun-loving, active, accepting, and kind person. Suddenly, she seemed to stop caring about playing the violin, even though she used to love it. She stopped being an upstander, too. Carly now spent a lot of time laughing about others with her new friends, excluding others who tried to sit near her new group, and Maya even heard her old friend gossiping negatively about a classmate's science presentation.

Maya didn't recognize Carly's personality anymore. She felt that Carly had changed so much that she had to end their friendship. Maya said to Carly, "I know I'll miss you, but you don't seem to value our friendship anymore and you have really changed. If you ever want to be friends again, and act like your old self, I'm here for you. In the meantime, I'm going to make new friends, too."

Carly felt that Maya was acting superior and being annoying. Carly decided that they would never be friends again. Both girls, though, privately missed their connection.

- ° If you were Carly or Maya, what would you have done in this changing situation?
- ° Do you think that Maya should have remained quiet or should have spoken up the way she did?
- ° What would you do if, like Carly, you were feeling the temptation to change just to be accepted?

If your friendship ends, you may find that you miss the person. You may miss your talks, your activities, or just knowing that your friend was there for you. Be cautious before permanently walking away from a long-term friendship.

Remember, a good friend builds you up and helps you to feel accepted and supported.

There are times when people question whether it's worth keeping a friendship. For example, maybe you don't see each other as often, or you are always the one to compromise on what you do together. If the friendship is hurting you—if your friend now embarrasses you or makes you feel bad—it may be time to have a conversation about what you need or want, and what you feel is hurtful, in the friendship. You may even decide to take a friendship break. This can be difficult, and you may feel sad or angry, but someone who makes you feel bad isn't really being a good friend. Remember, a good friend builds you up and helps you to feel accepted and supported.

Sometimes you may not be the one to decide if a long-term friendship ends. The other person may be the one to end it. Why? Over time, your friend might have started to want something different out of friendships, especially if you both have changed. Or maybe you just grew apart after spending less time together. Perhaps the friendship needs to change but can still be maintained.

If you aren't spending as much time with a longtime friend anymore, or the friendship has ended, remind yourself regularly of why you are special and all the qualities that make you a good person and good friend. Enjoy time with your other friends and think about what you can have fun doing with new friends.

Call to Action

Think about your longtime friend. What keeps the two of you connected? Perhaps it's the activities you do together, or the talks you have and values you share. Maybe it's your similar sense of humor. Think about some specific ways you can maintain this special connection as you grow up. It may be easy, as you may continue to share things in common as you get older. Or it may be a bit of a challenge. If it is hard, remember why you became friends as you work on staying connected. If you want to have new friends, think about how you can stay close with your old friend while expanding your social network.

CONCLUSION

Now that you've read this book, hopefully you have a better understanding of how to make and keep friends, and how to be a good friend to others. If you are caring, respectful, and willing to compromise, you're on the right track. You should probably also look for these same characteristics in potential friends.

Remember to take your time to get to know someone. Close friendships, and certainly best friendships, don't usually develop overnight. It takes time to learn about and trust people. Give yourself time to get to know the other person and give the other person time to get to know you and all your special qualities.

Friendship can sometimes be challenging. Sometimes you and your friend may have a disagreement, different opinions, or some different interests. You may need to respectfully and calmly talk out an issue so that you and your friend are both heard and can look for solutions. The good news is that not every disagreement leads to the end of a friendship. Sometimes talking over the conflict can help both of you to understand each other better!

Socializing over social media has pros and cons. Hopefully, you picked up some good tips in this book on how social media can keep you connected to others, but also how to navigate your way through the potential downsides of technology.

As you start new friendships, or continue old ones, think about whether you feel accepted, supported, and happy. Friendships are supposed to add to your life, not make you feel like you always need to pretend to be someone else or risk rejection. Find the right people to spend time with, and try to hold onto the special, positive connections you have if they make you happy, even as you grow and change.

Finally, when you need a reminder about being a good friend or making and keeping friends, refer back to this book to help guide you.

Best of luck!

Wendy L. Moss, PhD,
ABPP, FAASP, has her doctorate
in clinical psychology, is a licensed
psychologist, and is certified in school
psychology. She is the author of many
acclaimed books for young readers,
including *Stand Up!: Be an Upstander and
Make a Difference; Bounce Back: How to
Be a Resilient Kid;* and *Being Me: A
Kid's Guide to Boosting Confidence
and Self-Esteem.*

Magination Press is the
children's book imprint of the American
Psychological Association. APA works to
advance psychology as a science and profession
and as a means of promoting health and human
welfare. Magination Press books reach young
readers and their parents and caregivers to make
navigating life's challenges a little easier. It's the
combined power of psychology and literature that
makes a Magination Press book special.
Visit maginationpress.org
 🅵 🅨 🅞 🅟 @MaginationPress